Existence and Divine Unity

from the Risale-i Nur Collection
Humanity's Encounter with the Divine Series

Existence
and
Divine Unity

- *The Twentieth Letter*
- *The Twenty-second Word*

Bediüzzaman
SAİD NURSİ

Light

New Jersey
2006

Published by The Light, Inc.
26 Worlds Fair Dr. Suite C
Somerset, New Jersey, 08873, USA

www.thelightpublishing.com

Translated from Turkish by Ali Ünal

Library of Congress Cataloging-in-Publication Data

Nursî, Said, 1877-1960.
  [Risale-i nur. English. Selections]
  Existence and divine unity / Bediuzzaman Said Nursi.
     p. cm. -- (Humanity's encounter with the divine ; 2)
  "From the Risale-i Nur collection."
  Includes bibliographical references (p.   ) and index.
  ISBN 0-9720654-7-4 (pbk. : alk. paper) 1. Nurculuk--
Doctrines. 2. Creation (Islam) 3. Islam--Doctrines. I.
Title. II. Series.
BP252.R5713 2002c
297.8'3--dc21

                                    2002013930

Printed by
Çağlayan A.Ş., Izmir - Turkey
January 2006

Table of Contents

Bediüzzaman and the Risale-i Nur ii

THE TWENTIETH LETTER

Aspects of Divine Unity

Introduction 2

First Station 3

[An analysis of eleven Qur'anic phrases dealing with Divine Unity]

Second Station 14

[A proof of Divine Unity at the level of God's Greatest Name]

Addendum to the tenth phrase 62

[Infinite ease in unity and endless difficulty in multiplicity and associating partners with God]

THE TWENTY-SECOND WORD

Arguments for Divine Existence and Unity and How to Acquire a Firm Conviction of Divine Unity

First station 71

Second station 73

Conclusion 132

Index 135

Bediüzzaman and the Risale-i Nur

In the many dimensions of his lifetime of achievement, as well as in his personality and character, Bediüzzaman (1877-1960) was and, through his continuing influence, still is an important thinker and writer in the Muslim world. He represented in a most effective and profound way the intellectual, moral and spiritual strengths of Islam, evident in different degrees throughout its fourteen-century history. He lived for eighty-five years. He spent almost all of those years, overflowing with love and ardor for the cause of Islam, in a wise and measured activism based on sound reasoning and in the shade of the Qur'an and the Prophetic example.

Bediüzzaman lived in an age when materialism was at its peak and many crazed after communism, and the world was in great crisis. In that critical period, Bediüzzaman pointed people to the source of belief and inculcated in them a strong hope for a collective restoration. At a time when science and philosophy were used to mislead young generations into atheism, and nihilistic attitudes had a wide appeal, at a time when all this was done in the name of civilization, modernization and contemporary thinking and those who tried to resist them were subjected to the cruelest of persecutions, Bediüzzaman strove for the overall revival of a whole people, breathing into their minds whatever and spirits whatever is taught in the institutions of both modern and traditional education and of spiritual training.

Bediüzzaman had seen that modern unbelief originated from science and philosophy, not from ignorance as previously. He wrote that nature is the collection of Divine signs and therefore science and religion cannot be conflicting disciplines. Rather, they are two (apparently) different expressions of the same truth. Minds should be enlightened with sciences, while hearts need to be illumined by religion.

Bediüzzaman was not a writer in the usual sense of the word. He wrote his splendid work the *Risale-i Nur*, a collection exceeding 5,000 pages, because he had a mission: he struggled against the materialistic and atheistic trends of thought fed by science and philosophy and tried to present the truths of Islam to modern minds and hearts of every level of understanding. The *Risale-i Nur*, a modern commentary of the Qur'an, mainly concentrates on the existence and unity of God, the Resurrection, Prophethood, the Divine Scriptures primarily including the Qur'an, the invisible realms of existence, Divine Destiny and humanity's free will, worship, justice in human life, and humanity's place and duty among the creation.

In order to remove from people's minds and hearts the accumulated 'sediment' of false beliefs and conceptions and to purify them both intellectually and spiritually, Bediüzzaman writes forcefully and makes reiterations. He writes in neither an academic nor a didactic way; rather he appeals to feelings and aims to pour out his thoughts and ideas into people's hearts and minds in order to awaken them to belief and conviction.

This book includes selected sections from the *Risale-i Nur* collection.

Aspects of
Divine Unity

In His Name, Glory be to Him.

There is nothing that does not glorify
Him with praise.

In the Name of God,
the Merciful, the Compassionate.

There is no god but God, One having no partner;
His is the Kingdom and to Him belongs all praise;
He alone gives life and makes to die; He is living
and dies not; in His hand is all good. He is powerful over everything, and unto Him is the home-
coming.

It is very meritorious to recite these affirma-
tions of Divine Unity after the day's first and last
prayers. Each phrase is equal in worth to God's
Greatest Name, and conveys good tidings to humanity by displaying and manifesting a different aspect
of the Lordship's Unity. This is equal to mani-

festing one of the Greatest Names, a ray of Divine
Singularity's magnificence, and a perfection of
Divine Oneness. Referring the reader to The Words
for a full explanation of such a sublime truth, I
summarize it below in an introduction and two
stations.[1]

Introduction

Belief in God is creation's highest aim and most
sublime result, and humanity's most exalted rank
is knowledge of Him. The most radiant happiness
and sweetest bounty for jinn and humanity is love
of God contained within knowledge of God. The
human spirit's purest joy and the human heart's
sheerest delight is spiritual ecstasy contained within love of God. All true happiness, pure joy, sweet
bounties, and unclouded pleasures are contained
within knowledge and love of God. Those who
truly know and love God can receive endless happiness, bounties, enlightenment, and mysteries.
Those who do not are afflicted with endless spiritual and material misery, pain, and fear. If any person were allowed to rule this world, despite his or
her being powerless, miserable, and unprotected

---

[1] Nursi, S., *The Words*, The Light, Inc., NJ: 2005.

amid other purposeless people in this world, what would its true worth be?

People who do not recognize their Owner and discover their Master are miserable and bewildered. But those who do, and then take refuge in His Mercy and rely on His Power, see this desolate world transformed into a place of rest and felicity, a place of exchange for the Hereafter.

First station

Each phrase affirming Divine Unity bears good tidings to believers. Each message offers a cure, and each cure contains a spiritual pleasure.

FIRST PHRASE: *There is no god but God* provides an inexhaustible source of help for the human spirit, which is subject to innumerable needs and prey to countless attacks, by opening the door to a treasury of mercy that can meet its needs. The spirit finds therein a point of support that shows and makes known its Master and Owner, its Creator and True Object of Worship, Who secures it against its enemies' evil.

This phrase saves the heart from desolation and the spirit from suffering through constant uplift and continual felicity.

SECOND PHRASE: *(He is) One* implies that the human spirit, which is connected to most species in the universe and thereby overwhelmed with misery and confusion, finds therein a refuge and savior to deliver it from such misery and confusion.

For humanity, the phrase means: God is One, so do not tire yourself with other things. Do not demean yourself and feel obliged to them, or humiliate yourself before them for security. Do not trouble yourself by following them, and do not tremble before them, for the Sovereign of the universe is one and holds the key to and the reins of all things. His command resolves everything. Finding Him means that you obtain whatever you wish and are liberated from interminable indebtedness and innumerable fears.

THIRD PHRASE: *He has no partner* means that He is One and has no partner in His Divinity and Sovereignty, as well as in His Lordship, acts, and creating. In principle, a worldly king may have no partner in his sovereignty, but nevertheless his officials may be regarded as his partners in the execution of his sovereignty, as they act as intermediaries between him and his subjects. God, the eternal Monarch, has no such need and therefore

no partner in His Sovereignty. One thing can interfere with another only if He permits it. In addition,
His Oneness rejects any intermediaries between
Him and His creatures, and so everyone has direct
access to Him regardless of time and place.

This phrase informs the human spirit that
nothing can prevent any believer from entering
the Presence of the Majestic, All-Gracious, All-
Powerful One of Perfection, Who is the Eternal
Owner of the treasuries of mercy and bliss, and
presenting his or her petition. Finding His Mercy
and relying upon His Power enables believers to
attain perfect ease and happiness.

FOURTH PHRASE: *His is the Kingdom* means
that He owns the heavens and Earth—including
you—and that you work in His Kingdom. It also
implies: Do not imagine that you own yourself,
for you cannot administer your own affairs. You
cannot maintain your spirit and body by meeting
their needs and securing them against calamity.
You cannot avoid exhaustion and aging, because
you are subject to time and other erosive factors.
Therefore, do not suffer pain and torment without
reason. Somebody All-Powerful and All-Compassionate owns everything. Rely on His Power and

do not accuse His Compassion. Renounce grief
and anxiety and accept relief. Be rid of your trou-
bles and find serenity.

This phrase also means: This world that you
love, to which you are connected and which you
see in disorder and cannot put right, belongs to an
All-Powerful and Compassionate One. So return it
to its Owner and leave it to Him. Mind your own
duty and do not interfere with His acts. Do not be
troubled by what you cannot overcome. Be at ease,
for its Owner controls it completely and administers it as He wills. He is All-Wise and All-Compassionate, and acts for a wise purpose. So whenever
you are afraid, say like Ibrahim Haqqi: "Let's see
what the Master does—whatever He does is
always best—and observe His acts with complete
trust."

FIFTH PHRASE: *To Him belongs all the praise*
means that only God deserves praise and acclaim,
that everything is indebted only to Him. All bounties are His, for they come from His infinite and
inexhaustible treasury.

This phrase implies: The bounties (you now
enjoy) will never cease, for His Mercy's treasury
is inexhaustible. Your (current) enjoyment will

never cease, for every enjoyment you are granted is the fruit of infinite Mercy. And the tree of that Mercy cannot die, for each exhausted fruit is replaced with a new one. Furthermore, offering thanks and praise for what you currently enjoy increases it a hundredfold, since every enjoyment is, in essence, a favor from the Divine Mercy and therefore 100 times more enjoyable than the enjoyment by itself. If a glorious king gives you an apple, your pleasure at such a royal favor will be superior to the material pleasure of 100 or even 1,000 apples.

Similarly, this phrase opens the door of a spiritual enjoyment 1,000 times sweeter, since it makes you consider the bestowal of bounty, which leads you to recognize the Bestower and reflect on His merciful favors that pour out continually.

SIXTH PHRASE: *He alone gives life* states that only He gives and sustains life and provides all its necessities, and that life's sublime aims and important results are related to Him.

This phrase calls out: Do not bother to shoulder life's heavy responsibilities, or feel unease because the world is transient, or let life's insignificant worldly fruits make you regret that you came to this world. Rather, the "life mechanism" in "your being's ship" belongs to the Ever-Living and Ever-Self-Subsistent One, Who fulfills all life's needs and expenditures. Further, life's innumerable aims direct it to many important results, nearly all of which are related to Him. You are just a helmsman on that ship, so perform your duty properly. Receive your wages and be content with the resulting enjoyment. Ponder that ship's preciousness and its valuable benefits, and consider the magnitude of its Owner's generosity and compassion. Rejoice and give thanks, for performing your duty righteously will cause your life's results to be recorded, in one respect, as good deeds securing your immortal life in eternity.

SEVENTH PHRASE: *...and makes to die* means that He discharges you from life's duty, changes your abode from this transient world to an eternal one, and releases you from the burden of service.

This phrase announces: Good news! Death is not annihilation or going to non-existence, not an eternal separation or a chance event without an author. Rather the All-Wise and All-Compassionate Author is discharging you from service, changing your abode, and sending you to the everlasting happiness that is your true home. Death is the door to union with the Intermediate World, where you will meet with 99 percent of your friends.

EIGHTH PHRASE: *He is living and dies not* means that the Undying Object of Worship and the Everlasting Beloved, One Whose Beauty, Perfection, and Benevolence are wholly superior to their counterparts in this world and that arouse the love of all creatures, has an eternal life. One manifestation of His Beauty replaces all other beloveds. His eternal life is free of any trace of cessation or ephemerality, and has no flaw or defect.

This phrase proclaims to all conscious beings, whether human or jinn, and to all lovers: The Eternal Beloved will heal the wounds caused by separation from your loved ones. Since He exists and is undying, do not worry about those others. You loved them because of their beauty and goodness, grace and perfection. But these are only dim, shadow-like manifestations of the Everlasting Beloved's Eternal Beauty, which has passed through many veils. So do not grieve when they disappear, for they are only mirrors. When the mirrors are changed, that Beauty's reflection is renewed and becomes more radiant. When you find Him, you find everything.

NINTH PHRASE: *In His hand is all good* means that only He possesses all good and guides you to do good. Also, He records on your behalf any good and righteous deed that you do.

This phrase announces: O helpless people and jinn, do not cry out when you die: "Alas, everything we owned is destroyed and our efforts have come to naught. We have left that wide, beautiful world and entered this narrow grave!" Everything is preserved, for all your deeds and services were recorded. The One of Majesty, in Whose hand is all good and Who is able to do whatever is good, summons you to reward your service. He will keep you underground temporarily and then bring you to His Presence. How fortunate you are that you completed your duty and service, for your labor is over and you are on the way to ease and mercy. Having toiled, you now receive your wages.

The All-Powerful One of Majesty, Who preserves seeds and grains as records of last spring's activities and services and then unfolds and publishes them the following spring in the most dazzling, abundant, and benevolent manner, also preserves the results of your deeds. Thus He will reward your service most abundantly.

TENTH PHRASE: *He is powerful over everything* means that He is One and Unique and has power over everything. As everything is therefore easy for Him, creating spring is as easy as creating a flower, and creating Paradise is as easy as creating spring. The countless creatures He continually brings into existence every instant bear witness with innumerable tongues to His limitless Power.

This phrase implies: O people, your service and worship are not lost. A world of reward, an abode of bliss, has been prepared for you. An everlasting Paradise awaits your arrival from the transitory world. Have belief and confidence in the Majestic Creator's promise, the One you know and worship, for He never breaks His promise. His Power contains no defect, and impotence does not interfere in His works. As He creates your small garden, He also can create Paradise for you. In fact, as He created it and promised it to you, He shall admit you to it."

Every year we watch Him speedily revive Earth with perfect order and ease despite countless animal and plant species and groups. Such an All-Powerful One of Majesty fulfills His promise. Furthermore, since He annually creates samples of Paradise, which He has promised through all His revealed Books; since all His acts and executions are performed with truth and seriousness; since the perfection of all His works point to and testify to His infinite Perfection, which contains no flaw or defect; and since breaking a promise, lying, falsehood, and deception are the ugliest of qualities, we can rest assured that the All-Powerful One of Majesty, the All-Wise One of Perfection, the All-Compassionate One of Grace will fulfill His promise. He will open the gate to eternal happiness and admit you, O people of belief, into Paradise, the original home of your forefather Adam (and foremother Eve).

ELEVENTH PHRASE: *And unto Him is the home-coming* means that all people are sent to this world of trial and examination for specific purposes. After fulfilling these, they return to the Presence of the All-Munificent Master, Majestic Creator, Who sent them in the first place. Leaving this transient realm, they are delivered from the turbulence of cause-and-effect cycles and from the obscure veils of means and devices. After that, they will be honored in the eternal abode in their Compassionate Lord's Presence and meet with Him, without any veil, in His Everlasting Kingdom. Everyone will discover that their creator is the Worshipped One, Lord, Master, and Owner. Thus this phrase implies the following news, much happier than all the rest:

O people, do you know where you are going, where you are being driven? You are going to the sphere of Mercy, to the peaceful Presence of the All-Beautiful One of Majesty. A happy life of 1,000 years in this world cannot be compared to an hour of life in Paradise, and 1,000 years of life in Paradise cannot be compared to an hour's vision of His Countenance of utmost beauty. All the loveliness and beauty seen in this world's creatures, including the loved ones that so fascinate and obsess you, are only shadows of one manifestation of His Beauty and the loveliness of His Names. Paradise and its charms are merely manifestations of His Mercy; all longing, love, and attraction are merely flashes from His Love's light. You are going into the Presence of the One Eternally Worshipped and Everlastingly Beloved, and are invited to Paradise, His eternal feasting place. So enter the grave with a smile.

This phrase also announces: O people, do not worry or think that you are going to extinction, non-existence, nothingness, darkness, oblivion, decay, and dissolution. In fact, you are going to permanence, eternal existence, and the world of His Light. You are returning to your true Owner, to the Eternal King's Seat. You will rest in the sphere of unity and not drown in multiplicity. You are bound for union and not separation.

Second station

(This station is a brief proof of Divine Unity at the level of God's Greatest Name.)

FIRST PHRASE: *There is no god but God.* This affirms God's Oneness in His Divinity and His being the Sole Object of Worship. The following is a very strong proof of the Divine Unity at this level.

The universe, and especially Earth's surface, display a most orderly activity. We observe a most wise creativity and a most systematic unfolding, for everything is given the most proper shape and form. We also witness a most affectionate, generous, and merciful provision and bountifulness. Such factors display the necessary Existence and Oneness of an Active, Creative, Opening, Shaping, and Bestowing One of Majesty.

The continual decay and renewal of all existents show that they manifest an All-Powerful Maker's sacred Names and reflect Its lights; are works of that Maker's creative activity, and inscriptions of the Pen of His Destiny and Power; and are mirrors reflecting His Perfection's grace.

Just as the universe's Owner proves this greatest truth and most exalted degree of His Oneness' manifestation through all the Scriptures and holy Pages He revealed, all people of truth and perfection prove this same degree through their investigations and spiritual discoveries. Creation also points to this by displaying miracles of artistry, wonders of power, and treasuries of wealth despite its helplessness and poverty. Those who deny that Single One of Unity must accept innumerable deities or, like the Sophists, deny both their own existence and that of the universe.[2]

---

[2] Particularly in the eyes of Plato, anyone who looks for the truth in phenomena alone, whether he interprets it subjectively

SECOND PHRASE: *(He is) One* states God's Oneness at the level of His Unity's explicit manifestation. The following proves this level decisively. When we gaze upon the universe, the first thing we notice is the perfect order and sensitive balance prevalent throughout it. Everything exists within a precise order and a delicate balance and

---

or relativistically, cannot hope to find it there; and his persistence in turning away from the right direction virtually amounts to a rejection of philosophy and of the search for truth. Many a subsequent thinker for whom metaphysics, or the investigation of the deepest nature of reality, was the crowning achievement of philosophy has felt with Plato that the Sophists were so antimetaphysical that they have no claim to rank as philosophers. But in a period when, for many philosophers, metaphysics is no longer the most important part of philosophy and is even for some no part at all, there is growing appreciation of a number of problems and doctrines recurring in the discussions of the Sophists in the 5th and 4th centuries BC. In the 18th and early 19th centuries the Sophists were considered charlatans. Their intellectual honesty was impugned, and their doctrines were blamed for weakening the moral fibre of Greece. The charge was based on two contentions, both correct: first, that many of the Sophists attacked the traditionally accepted moral code; and second, that they explored and even commended alternative approaches to morality that would condone or allow behavior of a kind inadmissible under the stricter traditional code. (Ed.)

measure. Looking closer, we notice a continuous ordering and balancing. Someone continually revitalizes this order with perfect regularity and precise measurements. Everything is, as it were, a model to be dressed in countless well-ordered and balanced forms.

Studying it even closer, we notice a wisdom and justice behind that ordering and balancing. Every event has a purpose, and each one provides a benefit. A still-closer look indicates the existence of a power behind the wholly wise activity in all that we see, as well as a comprehensive knowledge encompassing everything with all its aspects and functions. Taken together, these reveal that an All-Powerful and All-Knowing One operates behind veils of order and balance, One Who orders everything according to a most sensitive balance and for a universal purpose and justice.

When we analyze the beginning and end of all things, especially of living creatures, we observe that their seeds appear to contain all of those creatures' parts and structures. Their fruits hold the creatures' meanings, as well as their recorded life-histories, in a filtered and concentrated form. The seeds might even be said to be coded collections of the principles according to which they are created; their fruits an index of the commands of their creation and growth.

When we look into the outer and inner faces of living creatures, we easily see an extremely wise power's free control and an effective will's fashioning and ordering. The power creates, and the will designs and fashions. All of them display, on account of their beginning, a Knowledge's instructions; on account of their end, a Maker's plan and declaration; on account of their outer forms, an artistic, well-made garment that the One Who does whatever He wills tells them to wear; and, on account of their inner forms, an All-Powerful One's well-ordered machinery.

Given this, no time, place, or thing is beyond the grasp of the One Majestic Maker's Power. The Power of an All-Powerful Possessor of Will organizes and directs all things and their functions. The ordering and grace of One All-Merciful and All-Compassionate makes them beautiful, and the One All-Affectionate and All-Bounteous embellishes them with ornaments. Those who are alert can see the order and balance, and the clearly visible acts of ordering and balancing, all of which demonstrate, together with His absolute Unity, One Who is Single, Unique, Sole, All-Powerful, Possessing of Will, All-Knowing, and All-Wise.

Everything contains an aspect of unity, and unity points to One. For example, the world is illuminated by one lamp (the sun), and so the world's Owner is One. All of Earth's living creatures are served with air, fire, and water, each of which is one and simple (not compound). That being so, the One Who employs and subjugates them to us is also One.

THIRD PHRASE: *He has no partner.* Since this is proven in the Twenty-second Word's First Station, we refer readers to it.[3]

FOURTH PHRASE: *His is the Kingdom* means that He owns everything—from Earth to God's Throne, the ground to the sky, the minutest particles to all heavenly bodies, as well as everything within both past and future eternity and within this world and the Hereafter.[4] He has the highest

_____

[3] Nursi, S., *The Words*, The Light, Inc., NJ: 2005.

[4] Past eternity is not just the starting-point of time and therefore essential for the existence of things. In reality, it is like a mirror reflecting all past, present, and future time. People tend to imagine a limit for past time, which extends through

and most comprehensive degree of ownership, and the greatest manifestation of Divine Unity. A very strong proof for these truths once occurred to me in Arabic. For the sake of that pleasant memory, I expound upon those phrases below:

His is the Kingdom because the macrocosm is like the microcosm; both are works of His Power and missives of His Destiny. He invented the macrocosm, making it a place of prostration and worship, and created the microcosm, causing it to prostrate. He built the former and made it His property, and invented the latter, making it a servant. His art in the former was manifested as a book, and His fashioning and "coloring" in the latter exhibited itself through speech. His Power in the former reveals His Majesty, and His Mercy in the latter organizes His bounties. His Majesty in the former bears witness to His Unity, and His boun-

---

a chain of things, and call it past eternity. But this is incorrect, as the following example shows: Imagine yourself holding a mirror that reflects the past on the right and the future on the left. The mirror can reflect only one direction at a time, for to show both simultaneously you would have to rise high above your original position and reach a point where both right and left unite, thereby making it impossible to call anything first or last, beginning or end.

ty in the latter proclaims that He is One and Unique. His stamp on the former is on all things having totality, and His seal on the latter is on each particular body and limb.

FIRST SECTION: As the macrocosm (the universe) and the microcosm (humanity) are His Power's works and His Destiny's missives, they show the proofs of His Oneness written with the Pen of Divine Power and Destiny.

Humanity displays, albeit on a small scale, the same well-ordered art seen in the universe. Just as the universe's art points to the Single Maker, humanity's microscopic art testifies to that Maker and demonstrates His Oneness. Just as humanity is a meaningful missive of the Lord, a well-composed ode of His Destiny, the universe is another well-composed ode written by the same Pen of Destiny but on a vast scale. Given this, how could anything or anyone other than the Single One of Unity place His stamp on people's faces, thereby giving them the same structure and appearance but making each one unique, or set His seal of Unity on the universe, all of whose creatures work with each other so closely?

SECOND SECTION: He invented the macrocosm and made it a place of prostration and worship. The All-Wise Maker created the macrocosm in a novel and wonderful form, and inscribed His Grandeur's signs upon it to make it a huge mosque. Within it, He created men and women as intellectual beings to read those signs, and with a disposition to bow before Him in worship and prostrate in wonder at His miraculous art and wonderful, originative Power. Given this, how can humanity worship something other than that Single Maker of Unity?

THIRD SECTION: He created the microcosm, causing it to prostrate. He owns the former and makes the latter His servant. The Majestic Master of Sovereignty made the macrocosm, especially Earth, in the form of countless concentric spheres, each one being an arable field in which He sows, reaps, and harvests crops throughout eternity. He unceasingly administers His property and causes it to work. He made the World of Particles or Atoms (the largest sphere) a field in which He sows and harvests the universe's crops with His Power and Wisdom, and then dispatches them to the Invisible World, from the Sphere of Power to the Sphere of

Knowledge. Earth (a medium sphere) is another place of cultivation in which He plants species every season and then reaps and harvests them. He sends its immaterial crops (results of every thing's life) to the immaterial World of the Unseen.

He constantly fills each garden (a smaller sphere) with Power and empties it with Wisdom. He causes all animate creatures (an even smaller sphere) to yield crops far greater than themselves. In short, that Majestic Master of Sovereignty makes all things as models and dresses them in ever-different ways.

Using the His art's weavings, He embellishes them with ever-new inscriptions to manifest His Names and His Power's miracles. Everything is a page on which He inscribes in countless ways His meaningful missives, displays His Wisdom's signs, and has conscious beings to read them. Having made the macrocosm a cultivated property, He created and endowed humanity with structures and organs, senses and emotions, and especially with a soul. He then implanted such desires, appetites, drives, and demands that each person is in infinite need of the whole of that vast property.

Given this, who or what thing or being could have free control over that property and be lord of its servants other than that Majestic Master of Sovereignty, Who made everything a cultivated property; Who appointed humanity (despite its physical insignificance) as a superintendent, inspector, tiller, merchant, herald, and worshipper in that vast property; and Who took men and women as His honored guests and beloved addressees?

FOURTH SECTION: His art in the former was manifested as a book, and His fashioning and "coloring" in the latter exhibited itself through speech. The Majestic Maker manifests His meaningful art in the macrocosm as a book, thus making the universe intelligible. As a result, people acquire all true scientific knowledge from it and write all scientific treatises according to it. This universal book of wisdom, based on absolute truth, is proclaimed in the form of the Qur'an, a copy of that vast manifest book.

Just as His perfect art is manifested as above, His coloring and His Wisdom's inscriptions in humanity open the flower of speech. In other words, His art is so meaningful, delicate, and beautiful that it causes the components of that animate being to speak.

That Divine art so colored humanity (the "fairest of forms"), that an immaterial, incorporeal, and yet organic thing—the flower of speech—opens within each person's material, corporeal, and solid head. Further, that Divine art equipped the power of speech and expression with the developed tools and elaborate abilities and faculties needed for it to evolve into the Eternal Sovereign's addressee. Thus the Divine coloring in humanity's essential nature opened the flower of Divine speech. Who or what else, other than the Single One of Unity, can do such a miraculous thing?

FIFTH SECTION: His Power in the former reveals His Majesty; His Mercy in the latter organizes His bounties. The Maker's Power, manifesting Itself through grandeur and majesty, creates the universe as a magnificent palace adorned and illuminated with the sun (its electric light), the moon (its lamp), and stars (candles). He makes Earth a laden table, an arable field and garden, and each mountain a storehouse, a peg, a fortress. He provides all things on a vast scale and in the form of that palace's necessities, thereby demonstrating His Lordship's majesty in a most dazzling manner.

Similarly, He displays His Mercy in the form of graciousness by bestowing His bounties on every living creature. As He sustains them through His Bountifulness, He adorns them with manifestations of His Kindness and Generosity. And so He causes huge bodies like the sun to proclaim His Majesty through His Names the All-Gracious, Great, reciting: "O Glorious One, O Great One, O Mighty One," while tiny animate creatures like flies and fish proclaim His Mercy, reciting: "O Gracious One, O Compassionate One, O Generous One." Who or what else, other than the Gracious One of Majesty, the Majestic One of Grace, can interfere in this macrocosm's creation?

SIXTH SECTION: His Majesty in the former bears witness to His Unity; His bounty in the latter proclaims that He is One and Unique. Just as His Lordship's Majesty manifested throughout the universe proves and demonstrates God's Unity manifested with all His Names, His Lordship's Bounty, which dispatches every living creature's regular provision, proves and demonstrates His Oneness or Uniqueness manifested with some of His Names on parts or particulars.

God is *Wahid*: all creatures belong to, look to, and are created by One God. God is *Ahad*: most of the Creator's Names are manifested in every individual thing.[5] For example, sunlight's reflection on Earth may be seen as analogous to Unity, whereas the sun manifesting itself in each transparent object and water drop simultaneously (by its light, heat, and the seven colors within its light) may offer an analogy to Oneness. In the same way, the manifestation of most Divine Names in each thing, especially in each living creature and above all in each person, points to Oneness.

Thus this section indicates that the Lordship's Majesty, which controls the universe, makes that huge sun a servant, a lamp, and a furnace for Earth's living creatures; the mighty Earth a cradle, mansion, and place of trade; fire as a cook and friend; clouds as water filters and a means of nourishment;

---

[5] It is very hard to render God's two kinds of manifestations, namely *Wahidiya* and *Ahadiya*, in another language. *Wahidiya*, usually translated in this book as Unity, means God's overall manifestation throughout the universe or on wholes with almost all of His Names. *Ahadiya*, usually translated as Oneness and/or Uniqueness, means God's particular manifestation of one or a few of His Names on particular things or on parts. This kind of manifestation gives each thing or being its own nature and identity, and causes distinction among creatures. (Tr.)

mountains as storehouses and treasuries; air as a fan for living creatures, all of which breathe; and water as a nurse to newcomers to life, a distributor of sweet drink supplying animate beings with the moisture necessary for existence. This Divine Lordship clearly shows Divine Unity.

Who but the One Creator can make the sun serve Earth's inhabitants? Who but the Single One of Unity can arrange the air and use it as a swift servant with many Earth-related duties? Who but the Single One of Unity can make fire a cook, and cause a tiny flame to consume thousands of tons of things? Every thing, element, and heavenly body points to the All-Majestic One by manifesting Its Lordship's Majesty.

Just as Unity is apparent on the horizon of Grace and Majesty, Bounty and Benevolence proclaim Divine Oneness on the horizon of Grace and Mercy. Each living creature, especially men and women, are among the highest works of the all-embracing Divine artistry, and contain developed structures and organs that recognize and appreciate, desire and accept, innumerably different bounties. In particular, humanity absorbs the reflections of all Divine Names manifested in the universe.

Like a focal point, all people display most of God's Beautiful Names and proclaim His Oneness together through the mirror of their essential nature.

SEVENTH SECTION: His stamp on the former is on all things having totality; His seal on the latter is on each particular body and limb. Just as the Majestic Maker's greatest stamp is on the macrocosm as a whole, His stamp of Unity is on each of its parts and species. Each person's (the microcosm) face and body demonstrates that God is One, so does each limb. In short, the All-Powerful One of Majesty places on all things a stamp of Unity bearing witness to Him, and on each a seal of Unity pointing to Him.

FIFTH PHRASE: *To Him belongs all praise.* Since the perfections observed in all creatures (occasions of giving praise and paying tribute) are His, all praise belongs to Him. All odes and acclaims, regardless of origin and time, are addressed to Him, for praise is caused by bounty and beneficence, perfection and grace, and because everything leading to praise belongs to Him. Indeed, the Qur'an points out that whatever a creature does or is seen to do is, in reality, its worship, glorification, prostration, supplication, and praise—all of which rise continuously to the Divine Court. The following comparison shows this truth affirming God's Unity.

We see the universe as a huge enclosed park, its roof gilded with lofty stars and its ground inhabited by ornamented creatures. In this form, we see its well-ordered, luminous heavenly bodies and purposeful and ornamented earthly creatures pronounce, simultaneously and in their particular tongues: "We are miracles of an All-Powerful One of Majesty's Power. We bear witness to the Unity of an All-Wise Creator, an All-Powerful Maker."

Viewing Earth as a garden containing countless varieties of multicolored and beautifully ordered flowering plants and through which innumerable animal species are scattered, we see them proclaim, through their well-ordered structures and well-proportioned forms: "Each of us is a miracle, a wonder of art created by a Single All-Wise Maker, a herald and witness to His Unity."

Looking at the upper parts of that garden's trees, we see knowingly, wisely, generously, and beautifully made fruits and blossoms. They proclaim with one tongue: "We are miraculous gifts and wondrous bounties of an All-Merciful One of Grace and an All-Compassionate One of Perfection."

Thus the park's heavenly bodies and beings, the garden's plants and bushes, and its trees' and vegetation's blossoms and fruits testify and proclaim: "Our Creator and Fashioner, Who has granted us such gifts, controls all things. Nothing is difficult for Him or beyond His Power, in relation to which everything is equal and has the same value. The largest is as easy as the smallest in relation to His Power; and the small is as full of artistry as the large. In fact, the artistry in the smaller is greater than in the larger."

All past events, which are wonders of His Power, bear witness that the Absolutely Powerful One brings into effect and existence all wonders of the future's contingencies. The One Who brought about yesterday will bring about tomorrow, the All-Powerful Being Who created the past will create the future, and the All-Wise Maker Who made this world will make the Hereafter. So, just as the All-Powerful One of Majesty is the true object of worship, He also is the only one worthy of such praise. As He is the exclusively Worshipped One, all praise and glory belong to Him.

Would the All-Wise Maker Who created the heavens and Earth leave people to themselves and without purpose, even though they are the Tree of Creation's most significant and perfect fruit? Would He abandon them to random cause and effect, thereby reducing His profound Wisdom to futility? Would a wise and knowledgeable being plant and care for a tree in order to prepare it for important purposes, only to leave its fruits to rot or for thieves or to scatter? Of course not, for the whole point is to produce fruit.

Humanity is the universe's conscious being, most perfect fruit, result, and aim. Given this, why would the universe's All-Wise Maker give humanity's fruits—praise and worship, thanks and love— to others? Doing so would nullify Divine Wisdom and the purpose for creating humanity, stain His Power with impotence, and convert His All-Encompassing Knowledge into ignorance.

Since conscious beings are the pivot of the Divine aims behind creating the universe, their thanks and worship given for the bounties they receive can be directed only to the Maker. One who cannot create spring or all fruits (which bear the same stamp) cannot create an apple, give it to someone as a bounty and grace, and then receive that person's thanks (sharing in the praise due to the only One Who deserves it).

Given this, the universe's Creator and Majestic Provider, Who sustains all creatures and makes Himself loved by conscious beings through His art's innumerable miracles, will not abandon their thanks and worship, praise and love, recognition and gratitude to nature and causes. Doing so would deny His Absolute Wisdom and nullify His Lordship's Sovereignty. All thanks and praise belong to Him alone, for the universe's reality unceasingly proclaims with the tongue of truth: "Every being, from past eternity to future eternity, praises Him."

SIXTH PHRASE: *He alone gives life* means that as only He can give life, only He can create anything, for the universe's spirit, light, essence, result, and cream is life. Thus the giver of life must be the universe's Creator and the One Who is Himself Ever-Living and Self-Subsistent. The comparison below proves God's Unity at this level of His manifestation.

We see the magnificent and innumerable armies of living creatures with their tents pitched on Earth's surface. Out of them, the Ever-Living, Self-Subsistent One sends a new and freshly mobilized army every spring from the Unseen world. This army comprises countless unique vegetable and animal nations. Although each one's uniform, provisions, instructions, discharge, and period of service differ, one Commander-in-Chief meets all their needs via His infinite Power and Wisdom, boundless Knowledge and Will, infinite Mercy and inexhaustible treasuries. There is no forgetting, confusion, or delay—only perfect orderliness and balance. He trains and demobilizes each according to its specific service and character.

Only the One with all-encompassing knowledge can know all particulars about that army. Only the One with absolute power can administer it and its necessities. Who or what else could interfere and share in this annual mobilization displaying resurrection and precise administration, in this training and sustaining?

Our [inherent] incapacity allows us only to equip a battalion in a single fashion, even if it consists of ten different tribes. But the Ever-Living, Self-Subsistent One easily provides each of His magnificent army's countless tribes with the equipment necessary for their life and does so in a most wise and exact order. He causes that mighty army to pronounce with one tongue: "He is the One Who brings to life," and causes that vast congregation in the mosque of the universe to recite:

> God! There is no god but He—the Living, Self-Subsistent, Eternal. No slumber or sleep seizes Him. He owns what is in the heavens and on Earth. Who can intercede with Him unless He permits it? He knows what is before and behind them, while they encompass of His knowledge only that which He wills. His Throne embraces the heavens and Earth, and it does not tire Him to uphold them both. He is the Most High, the Supreme. (2:255)

SEVENTH PHRASE: *He makes to die.* He gives and withdraws life. Death is not a destruction or extinction to be attributed to nature and causes. Rather, just as a seed outwardly dies and rots while inwardly growing into a new and more elaborate living plant, death is the beginning of eternal life. Thus the Absolutely Powerful One Who creates death grants and administers life. We point to a mighty proof of this display of Divine Unity below.

Divine Will causes existence to move in a continuous flow. For example, the universe moves incessantly by its Lord's Command. All creatures, by God's leave, flow unceasingly in the stream of time. Sent from the Unseen World, they are dressed in external (material) existence here and then orderly poured into the other world. By the Lord's Command, they continually come from the future, pause at the present, and then are poured into the past.

This ordered flow is carried out with the wisest mercy and benevolence. The consistent movement is done by a most knowledgeable wisdom and orderliness. The flow's current is managed with solicitude and equilibrium. Everything is done for definite purposes, benefits, and aims. In other words, an All-Powerful One of Majesty, an All-Wise One of Perfection continually gives life to and employs the families of beings, from their individual members to the worlds they form, and then discharges them for a purpose. He makes them die, sends them to the other world, and transfers them from the sphere of Power to the sphere of Knowledge.

One who cannot administer this universe and time, give life to diverse creatures and call them to death as single individuals, create spring as easily as a flower and plant it and then pluck it through death, cannot claim to create death and make living things die. A most insignificant living thing's life and death must occur according to the Law of an All-Majestic Being in Whose hand are all truths of life and varieties of death, and by His permission, Command, Power, and Knowledge.

EIGHTH PHRASE: *He is Living and dies not.* His life is perpetual and eternal, without beginning or end. Death and non-existence are meaningless to Him, because life originates in His Essence and is indispensable to It. He Who has no beginning has no end. He Who is Necessarily Existent is eternally enduring. How could non-existence befall a Life that renders all of existence its shadow? Non-existence and perishing cannot touch a Life that requires and is required by necessary existence. Cessation and extinction cannot affect a Life through Whose manifestation all lives come into being, on which the universe's permanent truths depend, and through which they subsist.

One of Life's manifestations gives uniformity to that which is subject to extinction and decrease in this world of multiplicity. Saving them from disintegration, it gives them a sort of permanence. In other words, life [in the universe, which is a manifestation of the Eternal Life,] gives a sort of unity to multiplicity and a form of permanence to existent forms [either through a species' life, seed, offspring or in other beings' memories.] As a result, ephemerality and transience have nothing to do with this Necessary Life, one manifestation of which causes innumerable instances of life.

The universe's transience and decrease bear witness to this truth. Just as existents bear witness and point to the Ever-Living and Necessarily Existent One's Life via their existence and lives, they testify and point to that Life's permanence and eternity via their decay and death.[6] The appearance of new beings after their predecessors' deaths shows that an Ever-Living One unceasingly renews life's manifestation. Bubbles on a flowing river come in great numbers, display the sparkle of the one and same sun, and disappear, while the new, succeeding ones display the sun's images. This

---

[6] While proving God's Existence, Unity, and absolute Sovereignty over the universe to Nimrod, Prophet Abraham argues that God gives life and causes death, and then mentions that He causes the sun to rise in the east and set in the west (2:258). This transition from a particular to a universal meaning of giving life and death demonstrates that proof's most illuminating and widest sphere. It is not, as some interpreters of the Qur'an assert, a transition from an implicit to an explicit proof.

points to a high and enduring sun's permanence. In the same way, the alternation of life and death in those constantly moving existents bears witness to an Ever-Living, Ever-Enduring One's permanence.

These beings are mirrors. As darkness is the mirror to light and the more intense the darkness the more brilliantly it displays the light, so do these beings act as mirrors to God's Names and Attributes through the contrast of opposites. For example, just as beings act as mirrors to the Maker's Power through their impotence and to His Riches through their poverty, they act as mirrors to His Permanence through their transience. In particular, soil and trees clearly reflect the Power and Mercy of One Absolutely Powerful and Absolutely Wealthy through their poverty during winter and their dazzling pomp and riches during spring. It is as if all beings supplicate in the language of their being, like Uways al-Qarani:[7]

_____

[7] Uways al-Qarani is generally regarded as the greatest Tabi'un [member of the first post-Companion generation]. Although old enough to have seen the Prophet, he had no opportunity to do so. One day the Messenger advised his Companions: "If you see Uways al-Qarani, ask him to pray for you." Muslim, *Fada'il al-Sahaba*, 223-24. (Tr.)

Our God! You are our Lord because we see that we are mere servants. We cannot train ourselves, so train us. You are the Creator, because we are created and being made. You are the Provider, because we need provision and cannot provide for ourselves. Thus You make and provide for us. You are the true Owner, because we are owned. We do not have total control over ourselves, so You are the Owner.

You are the Mighty, having dignity and grandeur. Looking at ourselves, we see a mightiness manifested through us despite our poverty and helplessness. So we are mirrors to Your Sublimity and Might. You are the Absolutely Wealthy, and we are poor but granted riches that we cannot obtain by ourselves. Thus You are the Wealthy, the Giver.

You are Ever-Living, Ever-Permanent, because we are born and die and thereby see the manifestation of a perpetual Giver of Life. You are Ever-Permanent, because we see Your continuation and permanence in our demise and transience. You answer us and grant us gifts because we, all creatures, always call out and request, either through words or in the language of our ways of being. All our desires are satisfied, our aims achieved. Thus You answer our pleas.

Every creature is a mirror having the meaning of supplication and reflecting Divine Power and Perfection through its helplessness, poverty, and deficiency.

NINTH PHRASE: *In His hand is all good* means that all good deeds are in His Book and all benevolence is in His Treasury. Given this, those who desire good must seek it from Him, and those who desire what is best must entreat Him. To show this truth, we present the following instance of Divine Knowledge:

The Maker Who creates and exerts authority in this universe, as observed through His acts, has an All-Encompassing Knowledge inherent to His Essence. Just as this All-Encompassing Knowl-edge is indispensable to that Being—as the sun cannot be thought of without its light—it is essential to all things because it envelopes their being. Just as objects on Earth's surface see the sun, nothing can be hidden from the light of that Knowledge, Which encompasses and penetrates all things.

If that solid sun, those unconscious X-rays, and whatever else which is a source of light, as well as helpless humanity, can see and penetrate whatever faces them, despite being contingent, defective, and accidental, how can anything be hidden from the light of that necessarily all-encompassing and essential Eternal Knowledge? Countless signs point to this truth, as seen below:

All wisdom witnessed in all beings points to that Knowledge, for He Who acts out of kindness and graciousness does so because He knows. All well-ordered creatures, each of which has a precise balance, a balanced and measured form, and a perfect order, point to that All-Encompassing Knowledge, for order requires knowledge. All graces and adornments display knowledge. The artist who works according to a strict measure and balance relies on a powerful knowledge. Each creature's precise proportions, its shape determined according to its purpose and benefits, and its fruitful conditions and compositions indicate that they are made according to the principles of Divine Decree and the compasses of Divine Determination. They all show His All-Encompassing Knowledge.

Only one with an all-encompassing knowledge can give each thing a unique yet well-ordered form appropriate to and relevant for its life and existence. Only one with an all-encompassing knowledge can meet all living creatures' needs in a suitable way, at the appropriate time, and from unexpected places. Only the One Who knows each thing's needs can meet them.

As each creature will die, its ignorance of when this will occur shows that death depends on a law of determination and displays an all-encompassing knowledge. Although it does not appear so at first sight, everything—particularly plants—will die at an appointed time. These things' seeds and offspring are preserved to continue their duties or functions, to be the means of transformation into new lives. This also demonstrates an all-encompassing knowledge.

Each being is gratified by Mercy, Which encompasses all beings, for the One Who feeds sentient creatures' offspring with milk and sustains Earth's vegetation with water and rain must know the needs of all infants and vegetation. This points to a comprehensive knowledge. The care seen in making all creatures, as well as their artistic design and skillful adornment, displays an all-encompassing knowledge, for only such knowledge can choose an orderly, adorned, artistic, and purposeful state from countless possible states.

The perfect ease in creating and originating things points to perfect knowledge, for ease and facility of achievement are directly proportional to the degree of knowledge and skill. The more one knows about something, the more easily one accomplishes it. We can see how all things, each a miracle of art, are created quickly and miraculously with astonishing ease and facility.

In addition, thousands of other true signs show that the One Who controls the universe has an all-encompassing knowledge. He knows all things' qualities and functions, and then acts. Since the universe's Owner has such knowledge, He sees us and our actions and rewards and punishes us accordingly. He deals—and will deal—with us according to the requirements of His Wisdom and Mercy. So be sensible! Think carefully of this Being Who knows and watches you. Realize these truths and pull yourself together.

A POSSIBLE OBJECTION: If you say that Knowledge alone is not sufficient, for Will is also necessary, I reply: All creatures bear witness to Divine All-Encompassing Knowledge, and point to the universal Will of the One with that Knowledge.

A universal Will is demonstrated in many ways: Each creature, especially sentient beings, hesitates among many possibilities and yet receives a most well-ordered and specific identity through one probability determined from many, and through a certain way leading to one result out of many fruit-less ways. This well-ordered identity, measure, and form are given according to a most sensitive scale and subtle organization, and are cut from solid elements flowing randomly in endless possibilities and fruitless ways. This shows that they are the works of a universal Will, for choice happens only through designation, preference, purpose and will, specification, deliberate intention and desire. Specifying requires one who specifies, and preference requires one who prefers. Only the Will specifies and prefers.

For example, a person resembles a machine composed of hundreds of systems and components, although he or she is created from a drop of water. A bird and a tree, both of which have hundreds of parts, are created from a simple egg and a simple seed, respectively. Such things testify to Power and Knowledge and indicate their Maker's Universal Will, with which He specifies each being's members, parts, and unique shape.

In short, just as the resemblance and correspondence between an animal's major bodily parts with respect to their basic aspects and results indicate their Maker's Oneness, their unique identities and faces prove that their Maker of Unity has Will and absolute freedom in His acts. He does only what He wills to do, acts independently of the universe, and has an absolute, universal Will. Thus each creature, or each function of each creature, testifies to Divine Knowledge and Will. Given this, those who deny Divine Destiny, who claim that Divine Knowledge does not comprehend all particulars or that the existence of some creatures is due to natural cause and effect, are seriously mistaken and deluded. Their denial is a lie of infinite dimensions. So, consider how mistaken and contrary to the truth it is to say "naturally" of any event, for all occur through Divine Will. Rather, say: "If God wills."

TENTH PHRASE: *He is powerful over everything.* As everything is easy for Him, He easily clothes everything with existence and creates everything by saying: *"Be."*

If a very skillful artist only has to stretch out a hand to make something and everything operate as he or she wills, we may express such speed and skill by saying that the artist controls that work to such a degree that it seems to come into existence by a single touch or command. *His command when*

He wills a thing, is only to say to it "Be" and it is (36:82) also declares that the Power of the All-Powerful One of Majesty controls every-thing and operates with utmost ease. The following five points explain five of this comprehensive truth's countless mysteries.

FIRST POINT: The greatest and the smallest thing are equal for Divine Power. Creating a species is as simple as creating an individual, creating Paradise is as easy as creating spring, and creating spring is as easy as creating a flower. This mystery has been explained in The Tenth Word and The Twenty-ninth Word, which prove that Divine Power creates stars, particles, and all individuals as easily as one individual.[8]

SECOND POINT: Animals and vegetation, which contain infinite multiplicity and liberality, display the highest degree of mastery and artistry, the greatest degree of distinction and differentiation within utmost profusion and intermingling, and the high-

---

[8] Nursi, S., *The Words*. The Tenth Word deals with the Resurrection, while The Twenty-ninth Word explains the mystery of creation's ease through luminosity, transparency, reciprocity, balance, orderliness, obedience, and abstraction. (Ed.)

est degree of artistry and beauty of creation with the greatest abundance and profusion. Furthermore, although their creation seems to require vast amounts of machinery and time, they are made with utmost ease and speed, as if suddenly and out of nothing. This seasonal activity proves that size and number do not affect Power's ability to create.

THIRD POINT: The All-Powerful Maker's Power creates the highest universal as easily as the smallest particular, and with the same artistic value, due to the assistance coming from Divine Unity, the facility originating in the unity of the center governing the universe, and the manifestation of Divine Uniqueness or Oneness.

The assistance coming from Divine Unity— God's universal disposal through the overall manifestation of His Names: If one being owns and commands all things, such oneness enables him to concentrate the power of all things behind one thing and so manage all things as easily as one thing. Consider the following comparison:

A king, being the country's sole authority, can mobilize the army's moral strength behind every soldier. This enables a soldier to capture another king and command him in the king's name. Being the sole sovereign, that king also can manage the army and officials as easily as he uses one soldier and administers one official. As administrative power belongs to him alone, he can send everyone to aid one soldier, which allows each soldier to rely on all soldiers. But if his unique sovereignty and authority are nullified, each soldier would lose his limitless strength and become a weak, ordinary individual. And, administering them would cause as many difficulties as the number of soldiers.

Similarly, the Oneness of the universe's Maker allows Him to concentrate the manifestation of all His Names operating on all things together upon one thing, thereby creating it with infinite and valuable art. He causes all things to help, thereby strengthening other things when necessary. Through His Unity, He also creates, controls, and administers all things as if they were one thing. This Divine Unity ensures that the universe contains the highest degree of art and value within utmost abundance and variety.

The facility originating in the unity of the center: Everything becomes easy if things are managed from one center, by one hand and one law. For example, applying this to equipping an army, it becomes as easy to equip all soldiers as it is to equip one soldier. Otherwise, equipping one soldier is as difficult as equipping an army. Also, thousands of fruits easily grow on a tree that depends on one law and one root. But if only one fruit could be grown on each tree, it would be as hard to produce a fruit as it is to grow a tree. It also would require the presence of all elements necessary for the tree to live.

Thus, because the universe's Maker is Single and One, He acts through Unity. Given this, all things are as easy for Him as one thing, and He makes one thing as artistically valuable as all things. Furthermore, by creating a limitless profusion of valuable individuals, through the tongue of boundless abundance, He displays His absolute liberality and manifests His infinite generosity and creativity.

The display of Divine Uniqueness or Oneness: As the Majestic Maker is not physical or corporeal, time and place cannot restrict Him; nor can space interfere with His encompassing all things at the same time and witnessing all events; and means and mass cannot veil His acts. Both He and His acts are free of fragmentation or division. His acts do not impede one another, and so He does innumerable acts as if they were one act. Thus He makes a person contain a world, just as He encapsulates a huge tree in its seed, and directs and controls creation as if it were one person.

The sun's image is reflected in every burnished and shining object, for its luminosity makes it somewhat non-restrictable. Regardless of how many mirrors are held toward it, each one contains its complete, non-refracted image, without one preventing the other. If it were possible for everything to directly receive the manifestations of the sun—its image, seven-colored light, and heat—the sun could demonstrate its effects in each and every thing in all of its magnitude, and enter many places simultaneously as easily as one place. Similarly —*for God's is the highest comparison*—the Majestic Maker of the universe has, due to His Uniqueness, such a manifestation through all of His Attributes (which are pure light) and Names (which are luminous) that He is ever-present and witnessing everywhere, although He is nowhere. He does every act at the same time, in all places, and without any difficulty or obstruction.

It is due to these three means, namely, the assistance coming from Divine Unity, the facility originating in the unity of the center, and the manifestation of Divine Uniqueness or Oneness, that if creating and administering all creatures is attributed to One Maker, then they become as easy to create and administer as one thing only. Also, a single thing becomes as valuable in art as all things together. This truth is demonstrated by each individual's innumerable subtleties of art in the midst of creatures' endless abundance. If creation is not directly attributed to a single Creator, then creating each creature is as hard as creating all creatures, and the value of all creatures falls to that of a single creature.

This is why the Sophists, the most advanced in using reason among the philosophers, felt compelled to "renounce their intellects" and deny everything's existence. Realizing that the path of associating partners with God is infinitely harder to follow than that of the truth and affirming God's Unity and, because they already rejected the latter path, they fell into denial.

FOURTH POINT: Creating Paradise is as easy as creating spring for the Power of the All-Powerful

One Who administers the universe with readily observable acts. Likewise, a flower can be as delicate, beautiful, and valuable as a whole spring. This truth comes from three sources: the Creator's necessary Existence and total detachment from creation, the complete otherness of His Essence and His unrestricted Being, and His not being bound by space and His indivisibility.

First source: The Creator's necessary Existence and total detachment from creation cause infinite ease and facility. Consider this: Existence has varying degrees and levels, and so the worlds of existence are not the same. Thus a particle from one level deeply rooted in existence can contain a mountain from a less substantial level. For example, the mustard-seed-sized faculty of memory in a head belonging to the manifest corporeal world can hold as much as a library in the World of Meanings. Through reflection, a huge city is encompassed by a fingernail-sized mirror belonging to the external world.

If that memory and mirror had consciousness and creative power, they could use the power of their minute existence in the external world to be endlessly operative and bring about endless transformations in the worlds of meaning and reflection. In other words, an existent's power is directly proportional to the firmness of its establishment in existence. If existence attains complete firmness and stability, and thus complete detachment from corporeality and is therefore unrestricted, even its partial manifestation can direct many worlds belonging to less substantial levels of existence.

The universe's Majestic Maker is Necessarily Existent. His Existence is indispensable to His Essence and is eternal, for its non-existence is inconceivable and its cessation is impossible. As it is the most firmly established, fundamental, strongest, and perfect level of existence, all other levels are like pale shadows. His Necessary Existence is so deeply rooted and real, and the existence of all other beings (which are contingent) is so pale and insubstantial, that such discerning researchers as Muhiy al-Din ibn al-'Arabi conclude that only He really exists. Thus they reduce other levels of existence to illusion or the imaginary.

Given this, the Necessarily Existent Being's Power, which is both necessary and substantially related to His Essence, creates the accidental, weak, and relatively stable existence of contingent beings with infinite ease. To resurrect the dead for the Supreme Gathering and then judge them is as easy for Him as returning a tree to life every spring and causing it to yield leaves, blossoms, and fruit.

Second source: The complete otherness of His Essence and His unrestricted Being makes everything easy for him, for the universe's Maker differs from the universe. As His Essence is unique, no obstacle or restraint impedes Him or constrains His acts. He has complete and free control over everything. If managing the universe and its events were attributed to the universe itself, the resulting difficulty and confusion would prevent any form of existence and destroy all order and harmony.

For example, could the stones of a fine, vaulted dome fashion and arrange themselves, or a battalion be commanded effectively by the soldiers themselves? Even if such things were possible, everything would be in chaos. If the stones' arrangement is attributed to an artisan, and the battalion's command to an officer, both the artistic arrangement and the command are easy, for while the stones and soldiers block each other, the artisan and officer can deal with them from all sides and give orders without obstacle.

Thus the Necessarily Existent Being's sacred Essence differs from the essence of contingent beings. Rather, all truths are rays from the Truth, one of that Essence's Beautiful Names. Since His sacred Essence is necessarily existent, completely detached from materiality, and totally unique, that All-Majestic Being's Eternal Power easily sustains and administers the universe as if it were springtime or a single tree. Also, creating the other world, Paradise, Hell, and the Resurrection are as easy as resurrecting a tree that died last autumn.

Third source: The All-Powerful Maker's transcendence of space allows Him to be omnipresent through His Power. Being indivisible, He has total control over everything through His Names. As a result, His acts cannot be hindered by existent beings, means, and masses, for they have no need to do so. If there were some such need, then, like electric wires, tree branches, and veins, things would make His control easier, conduct life, and make His acts more prompt and speedy, rather than restricting, obstructing, and impeding such events. In essence, everything obeys and submits to the Majestic All-Powerful One's Power.

In conclusion, the All-Powerful Maker creates everything in an appropriate form without trouble, swiftly and easily, and without any process. He creates universals as easily as particulars, and particulars as artistically as universals. The Creator of universals and of the heavens and Earth is the Creator of particulars and the animate individuals contained therein, for those tiny particulars are the universals' fruits, seeds, and miniature specimens.

As particulars are like seeds and tiny copies of universals, He Who creates particulars must be the Creator and Controller of the universal elements and the heavens and Earth. If this were not so, how could He, in accordance with His Wisdom's principles and Knowledge's balances, make particulars encapsulate the contents, meanings, and samples of universal, all-encompassing entities?

As regards their wondrous art or the marvelous creativity they display, particulars are not inferior to universals. Flowers are not lower than stars, and seeds are not inferior to trees. Rather, the meaning of a tree inscribed in the seed by Divine Destiny is more wonderful than the actual, fully grown tree woven by Divine Power. Like-wise, creating humanity is more wonderful than creating the universe. If a Qur'an of wisdom were inscribed on an atom in some ethereal substance's particles, its value would surpass a Qur'an of grandeur written in the heavens' stars. Moreover, many particulars are superior to universals with respect to their miraculous art.

FIFTH POINT: The infinite ease and utmost speed in creating beings gives this firm conviction to the people of guidance: In relation to the Power of the One Who creates beings, it is as easy to create paradises, springs, and gardens as it is to create spring, gardens, and flowers, respectively. Also, as: *Your creation and your upraising are as but a single soul* (31:28) states, resurrecting humanity is as easy as making one person die and then live again. As stated explicitly in: *It will have been only one cry, then behold, they are all arranged before Us* (36:53), resurrecting humanity for the Supreme Gathering is as easy as assembling a dispersed army with one trumpet blast.

Although this utmost speed and ease prove the Maker's perfect Power, they have led the misguided to attribute the creation of things to the things themselves. Seeing that some ordinary things come into existence very easily, they mistakenly assume that they are self-created. They take what proves an infinite power's existence for proof of its non-existence! Through this mistaken attribution of perfection (e.g., infinite power and all-encompassing knowledge) to each particle, for all perfections are essential attributes only of the universe's Maker, they open the door to boundless possibility.

ELEVENTH PHRASE: *And unto Him is the homecoming.* Everything will return from the Realm of Transience to the Abode of Permanence and go to the Seat of the Ever-Enduring One's Eternal Sovereignty. Everything will transfer from the World of Multiple Causes to the Sphere of the Majestic One of Unity's Power, [where His Power operates without the veil of cause and effect]. Thus your place of recourse is His Court, and your place of refuge is His Mercy.

This eleventh phrase contains many more truths. Among them, the truth concerned with eternal happiness and Paradise is explained so clearly in the Tenth and Twenty-ninth Words that no need remains for further explanation. Both of those two Words convince the reader that, just as the sun that sets will rise again the following morning, life, this world's "immaterial sun," will rise to shine permanently on the morning of the Resurrection after it sets with the world's destruction. At that time, some jinn and human beings will be rewarded with eternal bliss, while the rest will be condemned to eternal torment.

Indeed, the universe's All-Wise Maker, Who has boundless All-Encompassing Knowledge, limitless universal Will and infinite All-Enveloping Power, the All-Compassionate Creator of human beings, promises in His Scriptures and decrees that believers will enjoy Paradise and eternal happiness. And so it will happen, for He does not break His promises, as doing so is a most ugly fault arising from either ignorance or incompetence. Since the One of Absolute Perfection cannot be sullied by any fault, or the Absolutely Powerful, the All-Knowing One by ignorance and impotence, breaking a promise is impossible.

Moreover, all Prophets, saints, scholars, believers—above all the Prophet[9]—continually request

_____

[9] In any publication dealing with Prophet Muhammad, his name or title is followed by "upon him be peace and blessings," to show our respect for him and because it is a religious

and entreat the All-Compassionate and Generous One for His promised eternal bliss through His Beautiful Names. Also, His Mercy, Compassion, Justice, and Wisdom (His Names: Merciful, Compassionate, Just, and Wise), as well as most of His other Beautiful Names (e.g., Lord and God) and Attributes (e.g., Lordship and Sovereignty), require the Hereafter and eternal happiness and testify to their reality. The Qur'an, His greatest Revelation, shows and teaches this truth, and Prophet Muhammad, His most beloved, taught it throughout his life and proved it through countless miracles.

> O God, bestow blessings and peace and benedictions upon him, his Family[10] and Companions, to the number of the breaths belonging to the people

requirement. For his Companions and other illustrious Muslims: "May God be pleased with him (or her)" is used. However, as this might be distracting to non-Muslim readers, these phrases do not appear in this book, on the understanding that they are assumed and that no disrespect is intended. (Ed.)

[10] The Prophet's Family: The Prophet, Ali, Fatima, Hasan, and Husayn. These people are known as the *Ahl al-Bayt*, the Family (or People) of the House. The Prophet's wives are not included in this designation. (Tr.)

of Paradise. Resurrect us and the publishers of this treatise, together with our friends, our companion Said, and our parents and brothers and sisters, under his banner. Grant us his intercession through Your Mercy, and cause us to enter Paradise in the company of his family and Companions, O Most Merciful of the Merciful. Amen. Amen.

Our Lord, do not take us to task if we forget or err. Our Lord, do not make our hearts swerve after You have guided us. Give us the gift of Your Mercy, for You are the Giver of Gifts. My Lord, open my heart and ease my task. Loosen a knot from my tongue so that people may understand my words. Our Lord, turn toward us in forgiveness, for You are the Acceptor of Repentance, the Compassionate. Glory be to You! We have no knowledge save what You have taught us. You are the All-Knowing, the All-Wise.

Addendum to the tenth phrase

In His Name, glory be to Him.

There is nothing that does not glorify
Him with praise.

In the Name of God,
the Merciful, the Compassionate.

Behold, it is only in (constant) remembrance of God that hearts are at rest. (13:28)

> God gives a parable: A man who is shared by many
> masters, each pulling him to himself. (39:29)

QUESTION: You proclaim infinite ease in unity and endless difficulty in multiplicity and associating partners with God. Thus it can be said that the ease in unity makes the existence of something necessary, while the difficulty in multiplicity makes it almost impossible. However, the difficulties and impossibilities you cite seem to be present with unity.

For example, [with respect to the existence of the universe] you say that if particles were not under the One God's Command, each particle would require an all-encompassing knowledge and absolute power, or would have to be able to command innumerable conceptual operations. But even if God controls all of them, do they not still have to have the same qualities to accomplish their infinitely orderly duties?

ANSWER: We put forward three brief allegories to reassure the soul and the mind about this truth, as follows:

FIRST ALLEGORY: In its own right, a tiny transparent and glistening speck cannot contain a light larger than its own dimensions and mass. However, if that speck is open to the sun's manifestation, it can comprehend that immense sun, its (seven-colored) light and heat, and so display a most comprehensive manifestation of it. On its own, a speck's functioning is limited by its dimensions. But if it connects to the sun by facing it and serving as a mirror, it can display examples of the sun's functioning to some degree.

Thus if each being's or particle's existence is attributed to nature, causes, or itself, each one must have the all-encompassing knowledge and absolute power or countless operative devices needed to perform its wonderful duties. But if existence is attributed to a Single One of Unity, each particle becomes His officer through the resulting connection. This enables it to manifest Him somehow and, along with being an object of His manifestation, depend on His Infinite Knowledge and Power. This relationship with the Creator's Power allows it to perform functions and duties far beyond its own power.

SECOND ALLEGORY: Imagine two people, one brave but self-dependent and the other patriotic and devoted to the country. When war breaks out, the first one wants to act independently of the state, and so carries the necessary equipment and ammunition on his back. Given his strength, he can engage only one enemy corporal in combat.

The second one, realizing his powerlessness, enlists in the army and becomes connected with the king. This connection enables the army to support him, and so he fights with the army's strength behind him. Encountering a enemy field marshal of the defeated army's king, he captures him in his own king's name. The first soldier must carry his equipment and sources of strength himself, and so can offer only an extremely insignificant service. The second soldier allows the army and the king to carry these. Just as though he were connecting his receiver through a tiny wire to the existing telecommunication network, this connection connects the second soldier to an infinite power.

If all creatures and particles are attributed and submitted directly to the Single One of Unity, they can use the resulting power and strength to achieve great feats. For example, an ant destroyed Pharaoh's palace, and a fly sent Nimrod to Hell.[11] In addition,

---

[11] This refers to the mosquito that entered through one of Nimrod's nostrils, thus causing the death of this tyrant who had cast Prophet Abraham into the fire. (Tr.)

a microbe can send an unjust tyrant to his or her grave, a wheat-grain-sized seed can produce a huge pine tree, and an air particle can enter all flowers and fruits in an orderly fashion. Such ease arises from that submission and being an officer. If everything is left to itself and, associating partners with God, attributes each creature's existence and operation to independent causes or to itself, then each creature's functioning is restricted to its own body and consciousness.

THIRD ALLEGORY: Imagine two friends who want to use statistical data to write a geographical work on a country they have never visited. One friend forms an intimate connection with that country's government. Entering the national tele-communication center and connecting his receiver to the state lines by a cheap piece of wire, he connects his telephone, communicates with every place and receives data, and writes an accurate and well-researched book. The second one [depending upon himself] would have to travel continuously for 50 years to see every place and obtain all the necessary data. Or, spending a vast sum of money, he would have to set up his own comprehensive telegraph and telephone system.

If countless things and creatures are attributed to the Single One of Unity, each connection becomes an object through which the "Eternal Sun" manifests Himself. This enables it to be connected with His Wisdom's laws, His Knowledge's principles, and His Power's laws. Through Divine Strength and Power, it rises to the rank of displaying a certain manifestation of the Lord and acquires an all-seeing eye, an all-looking face, and (all-important) words that have weight in all matters. Severing this connection reduces it to its own mass, for the universe is an organism composed of interrelated parts, and means that it would have to have absolute divinity to perform the functions described above.

The way of unity and belief represents such infinite ease that the existence of things becomes necessary, while that of associating partners with God has insurmountable difficulties. One being may arrange many things with great ease and in a particular way to obtain a certain result. However, this is beyond the ability of the things themselves.

The Third Letter says that ascribing the fine spectacles made by planets under the sun's "command," and Earth's yearly and daily movements that cause seasonal, diurnal and nocturnal cycles, to One Eternal Sovereign makes it easy for Him to use a "soldier" (Earth) to achieve this splendid result. Being told to "Move!" Earth rises with joy, whirls like a Mawlawi dervish in glorification of its Lord's Names, and the desired result is obtained easily and with perfect orderliness. If heavenly bodies tell Earth to move, the only possible result is chaos, even if millions of far larger stars set themselves in motion.

In conclusion, the Qur'an and believers attribute all creatures to One Maker and ascribe every affair directly to Him. Their way is so easy to follow that every creature's existence and every event become necessary. But those who ascribe one thing to innumerable causes follow such a difficult way that it becomes impossible. What is necessary for the coming into existence of one creature in the explanation of the misguided is sufficient for the creation of the whole universe in the explanation of the believer in the Qur'an. It is far easier for all things to issue by one command than for one thing to issue by innumerable commands. For example, an officer can command 1,000 soldiers as easily as one soldier, while 1,000 soldiers commanding one soldier would cause chaos, for it would be like commanding 1,000 soldiers separately.

This magnificent verse hurls this truth at those who associate partners with God:

> God gives a parable: A man who is shared by many masters, each pulling him to himself; and a man who belongs only to one master. Can the two be equal in comparison? Praise be to God! Nay, but most of them do not know. (39:29)

> Glory be to You. We have no knowledge save what You have taught us. You are the All-Knowing, the All-Wise. O God, bestow blessings and peace on our master Muhammad to the number of particles in the universe, and on his Family and Companions. Amen. All praise be to God, Lord of the worlds.

> O God, O Unique One, O Single One, O Besought-of-All. O He other than Whom there is no other god but Himself alone, Who has no partner. O He Whose is the Sovereignty and the Kingdom, and Whose is all praise. O He Who gives life and makes to die. O He in Whose hand is all good. O He Who is Powerful over everything. O He to Whom is the homecoming. For the sake of the mysteries contained in these phrases, join the publishers of this treatise, their friends, and its author Said with the perfected affirmers of God's Unity; the truthful, meticulous researchers; and God-conscious believers. Amen.

O God. For the sake of Your Oneness' mystery, make the publishers of this book spread the mysteries of Your Unity. Fill their hearts with the lights of belief and make their tongues speak the Qur'an's truths. Amen. Amen. Amen.

Arguments for Divine Existence and Unity and How to Acquire a Firm Conviction of Divine Unity

In the name of God, the Merciful, the Compassionate.

First station

Consider the following verses:

> God sets forth parables for humanity in order that they may bear (them) in mind and take lessons (through them). (14:25)

> Such parables do We set forth for humanity so that they may reflect. (59.21)

Once two people washed themselves in a pool and fell into a trance-like state. Upon awakening, they found themselves in a land of perfect order and harmony. They looked around in amazement: It appeared to them as a vast world, a well-ordered state, a splendid city. If it was looked at from still another point of view, it was a palace that was in itself a magnificent world. They traveled and saw its creatures speaking a language they did not know. However, their gestures indicated that they were doing important work and carrying out significant duties.

One of them said: "This world must have an administrator, this well-ordered state a master, this splendid city an owner, and this skillfully made palace a master builder. We must try to know him, for he brought us here. If we do not, who will help us? What can we expect from those impotent creatures whose language we do not know and who ignore us? Moreover, one who has made a huge world in the form of a state, a city, or a palace and filled it with wonderful things, embellished it with every adornment, and decorated it with instructive miracles wants something from us and those who come here. We must know him and learn what he wants."

The other person objected: "There is no such being to govern this world by himself," to which his friend replied: "If we do not recognize him and remain indifferent, we gain nothing and might face some harm. But if we try to recognize him, there is little hardship and the chance of great benefit. So how can we remain indifferent?" The other man insisted: "I find all my ease and enjoyment in not thinking of him. Besides, these things do not concern me. They happened by chance or by themselves." His smart friend replied: "Such obstinacy will get us and many others in trouble. Sometimes a state is ruined because of one ill-mannered person."

The other person turned and said: "Either prove that what you say is true or leave me alone." At that, his friend said:"Since your obstinacy borders on insanity and will cause us to suffer a great calamity, I will show you twelve proofs that this palace-like world, this city-like state, has one master builder who administers it and has no deficiency. He is invisible to us, but must see us and everything and also hear all voices. All his works seem miraculous. All these creatures whom we see but whose languages we do not understand must be his officials [working in his name].

Twelve proofs

FIRST PROOF: Look around. A hidden hand is working in everything, for something without strength is bearing loads weighing thousands of pounds.[12] Something without consciousness is doing much intelligent and purposive work.[13] As they therefore cannot be working on their own, a powerful, hidden one is causing them to work. If everything were happening on its own, all the work being done in this place must itself be a miracle, and everything a miracle-working marvel.

SECOND PROOF: Look at the adornments of these plains, fields, and residences. Each are marks pointing to that hidden one. Like a seal or stamp, each gives news of him. Look at what he produces from a few grams of cotton.[14] See how many rolls of cloth, linen, and flowered material have come out of it; how much sweet food and other delights are

---

[12] This refers to seeds, which bear trees on their heads.

[13] This refers to delicate plants like grapevines, which cannot rise by themselves or bear the weight of fruits, and so throw their delicate arms around other plants or trees and wind themselves around and load themselves onto them.

[14] For example, an atom-sized poppy seed, an apricot stone that weighs a few grams, or a melon seed each produce from Mercy's treasury woven leaves more beautiful than broadcloth, flowers whiter or yellower than linen, fruits sweeter than sugar, and finer and more delicious than jams, and offer them to us.

being made. If thousands of people clothed themselves from these or ate of those, there would still
be enough. Again, look. He has taken a handful of
iron, soil, water, coal, copper, silver, and gold and
made some living creatures.[15] Look and see. These
sorts of work are particular to one that holds this
land together with all its parts under his miraculous power and all-submissive to his will.

THIRD PROOF: Look at these priceless, moving works of art.[16] Each has been fashioned as a
miniature specimen of this huge palace. Whatever
is in the palace is found in these tiny moving
machines. Who but the builder of this amazing
palace could include all of it in a tiny machine?
Could chance or something purposeless have
intervened in this box-sized machine that contains a whole world? However many artistically
fashioned machines you see, each is like a seal
of that hidden one, like a herald or a proclama-

---

[15] This refers to the creation of animal bodies from elements
and living creatures from sperm.

[16] This refers to animals and human beings. Since an animal
is a tiny index of the world, and humanity is a miniature of
the universe, whatever is in the universe has a sample that is
contained within each human being.

tion. In their language of being, they announce: "We are the works of art of one who can make this entire world as easily as he made us."

FOURTH PROOF: I will show you something even stranger. Look. All things in this land are changing. Each lifeless body and unfeeling "bone" has started to move toward certain purposes, as if each were ruling the others. Look at this machine beside us.[17] It is as though it were issuing commands and all the materials necessary for its adornment and functioning were running to it from distant places. Look over there. That seemingly lifeless body is as though beckoning, for it makes the biggest bodies serve it and work for it.[18] You may compare the rest with these.

_____

[17] This refers to fruit-bearing trees. As if bearing on their slender branches hundreds of looms and factories, they weave wonderful, richly adorned leaves, blossoms and fruits, and then cook these fruits and offer them to us. Such majestic trees like pines and cedars have set up their workbenches on hard, dry rock to work.

[18] This "body" signifies grains, seeds, and the eggs of flies. A fly leaves its eggs on an elm tree's leaves. Suddenly, the huge tree turns its leaves into a mother's womb, a cradle, a store full of honey-like food, as if it, although not fruit-bearing, produces animate fruit.

Everything seems to have subjugated to itself all creatures in the world. If you do not accept the hidden one's existence, you must attribute all his skills, arts, and perfections to the stones, soil, animals, and creatures resembling people to the things themselves. In place of one miracle-working being, millions of miracle-workers like him have to exist, both opposed to and similar to each other at the same time, and one within the other, without causing any confusion and spoiling the order. But we know that when two rulers intervene in an affair, the result is confusion. When a village has two headmen, a town two governors, or a country two kings, chaos arises. Given this, what would happen if there were an infinite number of absolute rulers in the same place and at the same time?

FIFTH PROOF: Look carefully at the palace's ornaments and the city's adornments. See this land's orderliness and reflect on this world's artistry. If the pen of a hidden one with infinite miracles and skills is not working, or if all these ornaments are attributed to unconscious causes, blind chance and deaf nature, everything here would have to be a miracle-working decorator and a wonderful inscriber able to write 1,000 books in a letter, and to display infinitely different forms of artistry in a single ornament.

Look at the inscriptions on these stones.[19] Each contains the inscriptions of the whole palace, the laws for the city's order, and the programs for organizing the state. Given this, making all these inscriptions is as wonderful as making the state. So each inscription and instance of art is a proclamation of that hidden one and one of his seals. A letter indicates its writer, and an artistic inscription makes its inscriber known. Thus how can an inscriber, a designer, or a decorator, who inscribes a huge book in a single letter and displays 1,000 ornaments in a single one, not be known through his inscriptions and ornaments?

---

[19] This refers to humanity, the fruit of the Tree of Creation, and to the fruit that bears the program of its tree and its index. Whatever the Pen of Divine Power has inscribed in the great Book of the Universe has been compressed in our creation. Whatever the Pen of Divine Destiny has written in a huge tree has been included in its fingernail-sized fruit.

SIXTH PROOF: Come onto this vast plain.[20] We will climb to the top of that huge mountain to see the surrounding area. We use these binoculars, for curious things are happening in this land. Every hour things are happening that we never imagined.

Look! These mountains, plains, and towns are suddenly changing so that millions of new things can replace them with perfect orderliness, one within and after the other. The most curious transformations are occurring. It is as though innumerable kinds of cloths are being woven inside and among others. Familiar flowery things are being replaced in an orderly fashion with others of similar nature but different form. Everything is happening as if each plain and mountain is a page upon which infinite different books are being written without flaw or defect. It is inconceivable that these things, which display infinite art, skill, and exact-

_____

[20] This signifies Earth's face in spring and summer, when innumerable individuals of countless species are brought into existence and "written" on Earth. They are recruited and may undergo changes without flaw and with perfect orderliness. Thousands of tables of the Most Merciful One are laid out and then removed and replaced with fresh ones. All trees are like bearers of trays, and all gardens are like cauldrons.

ness, come about on their own. Rather, they show the artist who engenders them. The one who does all these things displays such miracles, for nothing is difficult for him. It is as easy for him to write 1,000 books as to write one book.

Look around you. He puts everything in its proper place with such wisdom, pours his favor so generously on the needy and deserving, draws back and opens general veils and doors so bountifully that all are satisfied, and lays out such munificent tables that a feast of bounties is given to all people and animals of this land. Indeed, the bounties are particular and suitable for each group and individual. How can all of this be attributed to chance, be purposeless or vain, or have many hands behind it? The only reasonable explanation is that their maker is powerful over everything, and that everything is subjugated to him. So, my friend, what pretext can you find to persist in your denial?

SEVENTH PROOF: Let's turn to the mutual interrelations of this amazing palace-like world's parts. Universal things are being done and general revolutions are taking place with such perfect orderliness that all rocks, soil, and trees in this palace obey this world's general rules as if each were free to do whatever it wills. Things that are most distant come to each other's aid. Look at that strange caravan coming from the unseen on mounts resembling trees, plants, and mountains.[21] Each member is carrying trays of food on its head and bringing it to the animals waiting on this side. Look at the mighty electric lamp in that dome.[22] It not only provides light, but also cooks their food so well that the food to be cooked is attached to a string by an unseen hand and held out and offered.[23] See these impotent, weak, defenseless little animals. Over their heads are small, spring-like "pumps" full of delicate sustenance.[24] They only have to press their mouths against these pumps to be fed.

In short, all things in this world, as if positioned face-to-face, help each other. As though seeing each other, they cooperate with each other. To perfect each other's work, they support each other and work

---

[21] "Caravans" of plants and trees bearing the sustenance of all animals.

[22] An allusion to the sun.

[23] The string and its attached food denote a tree's slender branches and the delicious fruits thereon.

[24] The breasts of mothers.

together. Their ways of cooperation cannot be counted. All of this proves that everything is subjugated to the builder of that wonderful palace, the real owner of this world. Everything works on his behalf, like a soldier carrying out his commands. Everything takes place by his power, moves by his command, and is arranged through his wisdom. Everything helps the others by his munificence, and everything is made to hasten to the aid of others through his compassion. O my friend, can you object to this?

EIGHTH PROOF: Come, O my friend who supposes yourself to be intelligent, as does my own selfhood. You do not want to recognize this magnificent palace's owner although everything points to him, shows him, and testifies to him. How can you deny such testimony? Given this, you have to deny the palace as well and say: "There is no world, no state." Deny your own existence, too, and disappear, or else come to your senses and listen to me.

In the palace are uniform elements and minerals that encompass the whole land.[25] Everything

---

[25] Elements and minerals denote the elements of air, water, light, and soil, which perform numerous systematic duties:

is made from them. This means that whoever owns them owns everything made from them, for whoever owns the field owns its crops, and whoever owns the sea owns its contents. These textiles and decorated woven clothes are made from a single substance. Obviously, the one who creates the substance both prepares it and makes it into yarn, for such a work does not allow the participation of others. Therefore, all of the things skillfully woven out of it are particular to him.

All types of such woven things are found throughout the land. They are being made all together, one inside or among others, in the same way and at the same instant. They can be the work only of one person who does everything with one command. Otherwise such correspondence and conformity as regards time, fashion, and quality would be impossible. So, each skillfully made thing is proclaims that hidden one and points to him. It is as if each kind of flowered cloth, skillfully

_____

By Divine permission, they hasten to help all needy beings, enter everywhere by Divine command and provide help, convey the necessities of life, and "suckle" living creatures. They also function as the source, origin, and cradle for the weaving and decoration of Divine artifacts.

made machine, and delicious morsel is a stamp, a seal, a sign of that miracle-working one.

It is also as if each is saying in the language of its being: "Whoever owns me as a work of art also owns the boxes and shops in which I am found." Each decoration says: "Whoever embroidered me also wove the roll of cloth in which I am located." Each delicious morsel says: "Whoever cooked me also has the cooking pot in which I am located." Each machine says: "Whoever made me also makes all those like me that are found throughout the land. The one who raises us everywhere is also the same. As this same person owns the land and this palace, he also must own us." This is because the real owner of, say a cartridge-belt or a button belonging to the state, has to own the factories in which they are made. If someone ignorantly claims ownership of it, it will be taken away. Such people will be punished for pretending to own the state's property.

In short, if each element has permeated through every other and encompasses the whole, their owner only can be the one who owns all the land. Since the instances of art found everywhere resemble each other and display the same stamp, whatev-

er has spread throughout the land is evidently
the work of a single person's art. And, that one rules
over everything. Thus there is a sign of oneness,
a stamp of unity in this magnificent palace-like
land. Some things are uniform, unique, and of the
same nature, yet all-encompassing. Other things,
though various and abundant, display a unity of
grouping since they resemble each other and are
found everywhere. Such unity declares the one
of unity. That means that this land's builder, host,
and owner must be one and the same.

Look attentively. See how a thickish string has
appeared from behind the veil of the Unseen.[26]
See how thousands of strings hang down from it.
See their tips, to which have been attached diamonds, decorations, favors, and gifts. There is a
gift particular to everyone. Can you be so foolish as not to recognize and thank the one who
offers such wonderful favors and gifts from
behind the veil of the Unseen? If you do not recognize him, you must argue: "The strings themselves make and offer these diamonds and other

---

[26] The "thick string" is a fruit-bearing tree, the strings are
its branches, and the diamond decorations, favors, and
gifts are the various flowers and fruits hung thereon.

gifts." In that case, you must attribute to each string the status and function of a king [who has a miraculous power and knowledge to do whatever he wishes]. And all this, while before our very eyes an unseen hand is making the strings and attaching gifts to them!

Given the latter fact, everything in this palace points to that miracle-working one rather than to itself. If you do not recognize him, by denying what is occurring in the palace, you show a determined ignorance of a kind to which a truly human being must not sink.

NINTH PROOF: Come, O friend. You neither recognize nor want to recognize the palace's owner because you deem his existence improbable. You deny because you cannot grasp his wonderful art and manner of acting. But how can all of these exquisite things, this wonderful existence, be explained without recognizing him? If we recognize him, all this palace and its abundant contents are as easy to understand as a single thing in it.

If we do not recognize him and if he did not exist, one thing would be as hard to explain as the whole palace, for everything is as skillfully made as the palace. Things would not be so abundant and economical. No one could have any of these things that we see. Look at the jar of jam attached to that string.[27] If it had not been miraculously made in his hidden kitchen, we could not have bought it at any price. But now we buy it for a few cents.

Every kind of persistent difficulty and impossibility follows from not recognizing him. A tree is given life from one root, through one law, and in one center. Therefore, forming thousands of fruits is as easy as forming one fruit. If this depended on different, particular centers and roots and on separate, particular laws, each fruit would have been as hard to form as the tree. If an army's equipment is produced in one factory, through one law, and in one center, it is done as easily as equipping one soldier. But if each soldier's equipment is procured from many places, then equipping one soldier would require as many factories as needed for the whole army.

This is also true in this well-organized palace, splendid city, progressive state, and magnificent

---

[27] The jar of jam denotes Mercy's gifts (melons, watermelons, pomegranates, and coconuts like tins of milk), each of which is a conserve of Divine Power.

world. If the invention of all these things is attributed to one being, it is easy to account for their infinite abundance, availability, and munificence. Otherwise everything would be so costly and hard that the whole world would not be enough to buy a single thing.

TENTH PROOF: My friend, we have been here for 15 days.[28] If we still do not know and recognize this world's rules, we deserve punishment. We have no excuses, because for 15 days we have not been interfered with, as though given respite. But neither have we been left to ourselves. We cannot wander about and cause disorder among creatures so delicate, well-balanced, subtle, skillfully made, and instructive as these. The majestic lord's punishment must be severe.

How majestic and powerful he must be to have arranged this huge world like a palace and turn it as though a light wheel. He administers this vast country like a house, missing nothing. Like filling a container and then emptying it, he continuously fills this palace, this city, this land with perfect orderliness and then empties it with perfect

---

[28] An allusion to the age of 15, the age of responsibility.

wisdom. Also, like setting up a table and then removing it, he lays out throughout the land, as though with an unseen hand, diverse tables with a great variety of foods one after the other, and then clears them away to bring new ones.[29] Seeing this and using your reason, you will understand that an infinite munificence is inherent in that awesome majesty.

Just as all these things testify to that unseen being's unity and sovereignty, so these revolutions and changes occurring one after the other bear witness to his permanence. How so? For the causes of things disappear along with them, whereas the things we attribute to causes are repeated after them. So nothing can be attributed to causes; everything takes place as the work of an undying one. For example, sparkling bubbles on a river's surface come and go, but new ones coming after them also sparkle. Therefore, what makes them sparkle is something constant standing high above the riv-

---

[29] The tables denote Earth's face in summer, during which hundreds of the Most Merciful One's tables are prepared fresh and different in the kitchens of mercy, and then are laid down and removed continuously. Every garden is a cooking pot, and every tree is a tray-bearer.

er and having permanent light. In the same way, the quick changes in this world and the things that replace the disappearing ones, assuming the same attributes, show that they are manifestations, inscriptions, mirrors, and works of art of a permanent and undying one.

ELEVENTH PROOF: Come, O friend. Now I will show you another decisive proof as powerful as the previous ten proofs put together. Let's board the ship and sail to that peninsula over there, for the keys to this mysterious world are there.[30] Moreover, everyone is looking to that peninsula, expecting something and receiving orders from there. We have landed. Look at the huge meeting over there, as if all the country's important people have gathered. Look carefully, for this great

---

[30] The ship refers to history, the peninsula to the place of Time of Happiness, and the age of the Prophet. Taking off the dress of modern civilization on the dark shore of this age, we sail on the ship of history over the sea of time, land on the Arabian peninsula in the Time of Happiness, and visit the Pride of Creation as he is carrying out his mission. We know that he is a proof of Divine Unity so brilliant that he illuminates the whole Earth and the two faces of time (past and future), and disperses the darkness of unbelief and misguidance.

community has a leader. Let's approach nearer to learn about him. See his brilliant decorations—more than a thousand.[31] How forcefully he speaks. How pleasant is his conversation. I have learned a little of what he says during these 15 days, and you could learn the same from me. He is speaking about the country's glorious miracle-displaying sovereign, who has sent him to us. See, he is displaying such wonders that we have to admit the truth of what he says.

Look carefully. Not only the peninsula's creatures are listening to him; he is making his voice heard in wonderful fashion by the whole country. Near and far, everyone is trying to listen to his discourse, even animals. Even the mountains are listening to the commandments he has brought so that they are stirring in their places. Those trees move to the place to which he points. He brings forth water wherever he wishes. He makes his fingers like an abundant spring and lets others drink from them.

---

[31] Thousand decorations signify the Prophet's miracles that, according to meticulous researchers, number around one thousand.

Look, that important lamp in the palace's dome splits into two at his gesture.[32] That means this whole land and its inhabitants recognize that he is an envoy. As though understanding that he is the most eminent and true translator of an unseen miracle-displaying one, the herald of his sovereignty, the discloser of his talisman, and a trustworthy envoy communicating his commandments, they heed and obey him. All around him, those who are sensible affirm whatever he says. By submitting to his commands and answering his beckoning, everything in this land, even the mountains, the trees, and the huge light that illuminates everywhere, affirm him.[33]

---

[32] The important lamp is the moon, which split into two at his gesture. As Mawlana Jami remarked: "That unlettered one who never wrote, wrote with the pen of his finger an alif [the first letter of the Arabic alphabet] on the page of the skies, and made one forty into two fifties." In other words, before he split the moon, it resembled the Arabic letter mim, the mathematical value of which is forty. After splitting, it became two crescents resembling two nuns, the value of which is fifty.

[33] The author refers to the mountains and trees answering the Prophet's call. See The Nineteenth Letter's ninth through twelfth signs in Said Nursi, The Letters (Turkey: The Light,

So, O friend, could there be any deception in the information brought by this most illustrious, magnificent, and serious of beings, who bears 1,000 decorations from the king's royal treasury? His words about the miracle-displaying king are said with total conviction and confirmed by all the country's notables, as is his description of the king's attributes and communication of his commands. If you think they contain some deception, you must deny the existence and reality of this palace, those lamps, and this congregation. Your objections will be refuted by the proof's power.

TWELFTH PROOF: You must have come to your senses a little. I will show you further proof as strong as the sum of the previous eleven proofs. Look at this illustrious decree,[34] which has descend-

Inc., 2002) (Tr.) The huge light is the sun. Once the Prophet was sleeping in 'Ali's arms, who did not wake him up out of deep love and respect for him. When the Prophet woke up, the sun was about to set, and 'Ali had not yet prayed the afternoon prayer. Upon the Prophet's order, Earth revolved a little backwards and the sun appeared above the horizon so 'Ali could pray. This is one of the Prophet's famous miracles.

[34] The illustrious decree refers to the Qur'an, and the seal to its miraculousness.

ed from above and which everyone looks upon with full attention out of amazement or veneration. That being with 1,000 decorations is explaining its meaning. The decree's brilliant style attracts everyone's admiration, and speaks of matters so important and serious that everyone feels compelled to listen. It describes all the acts, attributes, and commands of the one who governs this land, who made this palace, and exhibits these wonders. There is a mighty seal on the decree, an irresistible seal on every line and sentence. The meanings, truths, commandments, and instances of wisdom it provides are in a style unique to him, which also functions like a stamp or seal.

In short, this supreme decree shows that supreme being as clearly as the sun, so that one who is not blind can "see" him. If you have come to your senses, friend, this is enough for now. Do you have more objections?

The stubborn man replied: "In the face of all these proofs I can only say: 'All praise be to God,' for I have come to believe, in a way as bright as the sun and clear as daylight, that this land has a single Lord of Perfection, this world a single Owner of Majesty, and this palace a single Maker of Grace.

May God be pleased with you for saving me from my former obstinacy and foolishness. Each proof is sufficient to demonstrate the truth. But with each successive proof, clearer and finer, more pleasant, agreeable, and radiant levels of knowledge, scenes of acquaintanceship, and windows of love were opened and revealed. I listened and learned."

The parable indicating the mighty truth of Divine Unity and belief in God is completed. Through the grace of the Most Merciful, the enlightenment of the Qur'an, and the light of belief, I will now show, after an introduction, 12 gleams from the sun of Divine Unity, corresponding to the 12 proofs in the parable. Success and guidance are from God alone.

Second station

Consider the following verses:

> In the name of God, the Merciful, the Compassionate.

> God is the Creator of everything, and He is Guardian over everything; unto Him belong the keys of the heavens and Earth. (39:62-63)

So glory be to him, in Whose hand is the dominion of everything, and unto Whom you are being brought back. (36:83)

There is not a thing but its treasuries are with Us, and We send it down but in a due and certain measure. (15:21)

There is no creature that moves, but He takes it by the forelock. Surely my Lord is on a straight path. (11:56)

In my "Katra" (A Drop from the Ocean of Divine Unity's Proofs), which discusses belief in God, the first and most important of the pillars of belief, I briefly explained that every creature shows and bears witness to God's Existence and Unity in 55 ways. In my "Nukta," I mentioned four universals out of the evidences for Almighty God's Existence and Unity. In my [12] Arabic treatises, I discussed hundreds of decisive proofs for All-Mighty God's Existence and Unity. Thus I will not discuss the matter here in great depth, but only relate 12 gleams from the sun of belief in God. I have written about these briefly elsewhere in the *Risale-i Nur*.

Twelve gleams

FIRST GLEAM: The affirmation of Divine Unity is of two sorts. For example, if an important, rich man's goods arrive in a market or a town, their ownership can be known in two ways. One is to look at them and conclude that only he could own so many items. If a regular person estimated or supervised them, much might be stolen or others might claim partial ownership. The second way is to read every packet's label and recognize every roll's stamp and every bill's seal. This allows one to conclude that everything belongs to that person, for everything points to him.

In exactly the same way, there are two kinds of affirmation of Divine Unity. One is the believer's superficial and common affirmation: "God Almighty is One, without partner or like. This universe is His." The other is the true affirmation. By seeing His Power's stamp, His Lordship's seal, and Hispen's inscription on everything, one opens a window directly onto His light from everything. The person then confirms and believes, with almost the certainty coming from direct observation, that everything comes into existence by His Power's hand, that He has no partner or helper in His Divinity and Lordship or His absolute Sovereignty. Through this, one attains a degree of permanent awareness of the Divine Presence. I will now mention some "rays" to prove that everything shows God's Unity.

NOTE: Divine Dignity and Greatness require material or natural causes to veil Divine Power's operations. The real agent acting in the universe is the Eternally-Besought-of-All's Power. Divine Unity and Majesty, as well as God's absolute independence and transcendence, require this. The Eternal Sovereign's officials, all that conveys His commands (e.g., air, angels, or natural causes), are not executives through whom He exercises His Sovereignty, but heralds of His Sovereignty and, as with angels, observers and superintendents of His acts as Lord—Sustainer, Administrator, Upbringer, and Trainer—of the Worlds. They exist because they make known Power's dignity and Lordship's majesty, so that base and lowly things should not be attributed directly to Power.

Unlike a human king, who is essentially weak and destitute, God Almighty does not use officials to exercise His authority. Although everything seemingly occurs according to the principle of cause and effect, this is to preserve Power's dignity in the mind's superficial view.

Like a mirror, everything has two faces. One looks to the visible, material world, resembles the mirror's colored face, and may be a way to account for various "colors" and states. The other face is like the mirror's shinning face and looks to and consists of the inner dimension of things, where Divine Power operates directly. In the apparent, material face of things, there may be states that are seemingly incompatible with the dignity and perfection of the Eternally-Besought-of-All's Power. In this face, Divine Power veils His operations behind cause and effect so that those states may be ascribed to causes. But in reality and with respect to the inner dimension of things, everything is beautiful and transparent. It is fitting that Power should be associated with that dimension of things, which is not incompatible with Its dignity. Thus the function of causes is purely apparent, for they have no effect in respect to this dimension.

Another reason for apparent causes is that people tend to judge superficially. They raise unjust complaints and baseless objections about things or happenings that they find disagreeable. Almighty God, Who is totally just, has put causes in this material dimension of existence as a veil between such things or happenings and Himself so that such comments should not be aimed at Him. The faults and mistakes that make things and events disagreeable essentially originate in people themselves.

Here is a meaningful illustration of this subtle point: Azrail, the Angel of Death, once said to God Almighty: "Your servants will complain about and resent me, for I take their souls." God Almighty told him: "I shall put the veil of disasters and illnesses between you and my servants so that they will complain of them and not resent you." Thus illness is a veil to which people can attribute that which is disagreeable about death. However disagreeable in appearance, death is in reality good and beautiful, and the essential beauty lying in it is attributable to Azrail's duty. But Azrail is also an observer, a veil to Divine Power, so that people should attribute to him those aspects of death that their superficial reasoning cannot reconcile with Divine Mercy's perfection. Divine Dignity and Grandeur require that causes veil Divine Power's hand, while Divine Unity and Majesty demand that causes withdraw their hands from the true effect.

SECOND GLEAM: Look at this garden of the universe, this orchard of Earth. Notice the heavens' beautiful face, gilded with stars. Each creature scattered and spread out in them bears a stamp unique to the Maker, the Creator of all things. Each species bears illustrious and inimitable seals, all of which belong to the All-Majestic Maker, the All-Beautiful Creator, that are "written" on the pages of night and day, spring and summer, and published by Divine Power's Pen. I will mention only a few as examples.

Consider the stamp He placed on life: He makes everything out of one thing and one thing out of many things. He makes the countless members and systems of an animal's body out of fertilizing sperm-bearing fluid and also out of simple drinking water. To make everything out of one thing is surely the work of an Absolutely All-Powerful One. Also, One Who transforms with perfect orderliness all substances contained in innumerable kinds of vegetable or animal food into particular bodies, weaving from them a unique skin for each and various bodily members, is surely an All-Powerful and Absolutely All-Knowing One.[35]

---

[35] Countless beings eat the same kinds of food and are composed of the same elements, and yet each one has a unique face, fingerprints, character, ambitions, feelings, and so on.

The Creator of life and death administers life in this workshop of the world according to His Wisdom. He uses such a miraculous law issuing from the sphere (realm) of His Creative Commands, that to execute and enforce it is a function unique to Him Who holds the universe in the grasp of His administrative Power and absolutely unconditioned authority. Thus, if you can reason and have a heart that "sees," you will understand that producing everything from one thing with perfect ease and order, and skillfully making many things into one thing with perfect harmony and orderliness, is a stamp unique to the Maker, the Creator of everything.

If you see that, together with weaving 100 rolls of broadcloth and other materials like silk and linen from one dram of cotton, a wonder-working one also makes many foods from it like helva and pastries; and if you see that he skillfully makes gold out of iron and stone, honey and butter, water and soil, which he holds in his hand, you will con-

---

This is irrefutable proof of the Existence and Unity of an All-Knowing and All-Powerful Creator Who has absolute Will and can do whatever He pleases in whatever way He wills. (Tr.)

clude that he has a special art, a particular way of working, and that all earthly elements and substances are subjugated to his command and authority. Truly, the manifestation of the Divine Power and Wisdom in living forms is far more wonderful and amazing than this example. This is only one out of many stamps on living forms.

THIRD GLEAM: Look at the living creatures moving in this ever-moving universe, in these revolving bodies. The Ever-Living and Self-Subsistent One has placed many seals on each one. One of them is this: A person is a miniature of the universe, a fruit of the Tree of Creation, and a seed of this world, for each person comprises samples of most species of beings. It is as if each living being were a drop distilled from the universe with the most subtle and sensitive balance. To create this living being and be its Lord requires that the creator have full control over the universe.

Can you not understand that to make a honeybee (a word of power) a sort of small index of most things, to "write" on humanity (a page) most of the universe's features, to include in a tiny fig seed (a point) an entire fig tree's program, to exhibit in our heart (a letter) the works of all Divine

Names manifested throughout the universe, to record in human memory, which is situated in lentil-sized place, enough "writings" to fill a library, and to include in it a detailed index of all events in the cosmos, is most certainly a stamp unique to the Creator of all things and the All-Majestic Lord of the universe?

Thus if one seal of Lordship on living beings displays its light and makes His signs read in such a fashion, consider all those seals together. How can you not proclaim: "Glory be to Him Who is hidden by the intensity of His manifestation."

FOURTH GLEAM: Look carefully at the various multicolored beings floating in the heavens' "ocean" and scattered over Earth's face. Each one bears the Eternal Sun's inimitable signatures. Just as His seals on life and living beings are apparent, so are His signatures on His act of giving life. As comparisons make profound meanings more easily understood, I offer a suitable comparison. Consider the sun: From planets to drops of water, to fragments of glass and sparkling snowflakes, a signature from the sun's image and reflection, a radiant work (effect) particular to the sun, is apparent. If you do not accept the tiny suns apparent in these innumerable things as manifestations of the sun's reflection, you must accept the absurd statement that an actual sun exists in each item.

In just the same way, and with respect to the giving of life from among the Eternal Sun's manifestations, He has placed such a signature on each living being. Even if all causes came together and each one was a free agent able to do whatever it wills, they could not imitate that signature. Living beings (miracles of Divine Power) are each a focal point for the Divine Names' manifestations, which are like the Eternal Sun's rays. If, therefore, that amazing inscription of art, that curious composition of wisdom, that manifestation of the mystery of Oneness displayed by living beings is not attributed to the Single and Eternally Besought One, it means falling into total misguidance and superstition.

For example, it would mean giving each living creature an infinite creative power, an all-embracing knowledge, and an absolute will by which to govern the universe. In short, each one would have all the eternal attributes unique to the Necessarily Existent One. As such, each atom of that item would have to be divine, for each atom, especially seeds, are given such a character or properties that they take up a position in exact accordance. It is as if they are directly related with the whole species to which the living being growing from it belongs, for a seed seems to act in such a way that it is planted exactly in the place suitable for the continuation of its species and to plant the species' flag.

We may even say that the seed takes up a position so that the living being can continue its transactions and relations with all the other creatures with which it is connected to receive its necessary sustenance. If, then, that seed or atom does not act under an Absolutely Powerful One's command and its connection with Him is severed, it would have to have an eye with which to see all things and a consciousness encompassing all things.

In short, if the sun's images or reflections in water drops, glass fragments, and multicolored flowers are not attributed to the sun, we must accept the existence of innumerable suns. This is an inconceivable superstition. In the same way, if everything that exists is not attributed to the Absolutely All-Powerful One, we must accept the existence of as many gods as particles in the universe. Such an idea is clearly untenable.

In summary, then, each atom has three windows opening onto the Eternal Sun's light of Unity and Necessary Existence.

First window: A soldier has relations with all levels of an army, duties in accordance with those relations, and actions in accordance with those duties and army regulations. It is the same with each atom in your body. For example, an atom in your eye's pupil has similar relations and duties with your eyes, head, powers of reproduction, attraction and repulsion; with your veins and arteries, motor and sensory nerves that circulate your blood and work your body, and with the rest of your body. This shows that each bodily atom is a work of an Eternal, All-Powerful One and operates under His command.

Second window: An air molecule may visit, enter, and work within any flower or fruit. If it were not subjugated to and working under an Absolutely All-Powerful One's command, it would have to know all systems and structures of all flowers and fruits and how they are formed, down to their peripheric lines. So that molecule shows the rays of a light of Divine Unity like a sun. The same holds true for light, soil, and water. Science says that the original sources of things are hydrogen, oxygen, carbon, and nitrogen. All of these are the components of soil, air, water, and light.

Third window: The seeds of all flowering and fruit-bearing plants are composed of carbon, nitrogen, hydrogen, and oxygen. The only difference is the program of their progenitor deposited in them by Divine Destiny. If we put different kinds of seeds in a pot filled with soil, which is composed of particular or certain elements, each plant will appear in its own wonderful form, shape, and amazing members. If those particles were not subjugated to and under the command of One Who knows each thing with all its features, structures, lifecycles, and conditions of its life; One Who can endow everything with a suitable being and all that it needs; and to Whose Power everything is subjected without the least resistance, the following conclusions could not be avoided:

- Each soil atom would have to contain "immaterial factories" that determine all the plants' future lives as well as a number of workshops equal to all flowering and fruit-bearing plants, so that each could be the origin for these various beings. Do not forget that each plant differs in form, taste, color, and members.

- Each plant would have to have an all-encompassing knowledge and be able to form itself. In other words, if a being's connection with Almighty God is severed, you must accept a number of gods equal to the number of soil particles. This is untenable.

However, when you admit that the particles are working under an All-Powerful and All-Knowing One's command, everything becomes very easy. An ordinary soldier, in the name of a powerful king and by relying and depending upon his power, can force a whole people to migrate, join two seas [by having them build a canal], or capture another king. In the same way, by the Eternal King's command and permission, a fly may kill a tyrant, an ant may destroy another tyrant's palace, and a fig seed may bear the load of a fig tree.[36]

---

[36] A fly, entering Nimrod's nose and reaching his brain, caused him to die, and ants destroyed Pharaoh's palace.

Each atom contains two further true witnesses to the Maker's necessary Existence and Unity. Despite its absolute powerlessness, each atom performs many significant duties; despite its lifelessness, each atom displays a universal consciousness by acting in conformity with the universal order. Thus each atom testifies, through its impotence, to the Absolutely All-Powerful One's necessary Existence and to His Unity by acting in conformity with the order of the universe.

Each living being also contains two signs that He is the One and Eternally-Besought-of-All. In each is a seal of Divine Unity and a stamp of His being the Eternally-Besought-of-All, for each living being reflects in the mirror of itself all the Divine Names manifested in most parts of the universe. Like a focal point, it reflects the Ever-Living One's and the Self-Subsistent One's manifestations, two of the Greatest Divine Names. Since it reflects a display of the Unity of the Divine Essence behind the veil of the Name the Giver of Life, it bears a stamp of Divine Unity.

Again, since a living being is like a miniature of the universe and a fruit of the Tree of Creation, the easy satisfaction of its endless needs shows that God is the Eternally-Besought-of-All. In oth-er words, the being has a Lord Who is concerned with it and always cares for it. Such concern and care is far more valuable for it than everything in the universe.

[God's care] suffices a thing against everything, while all things [even if banded together] cannot suffice even a single thing against Him. This shows that the Lord of all beings needs nothing, that sat-isfying their needs does not diminish His Wealth, and that nothing is difficult for His Power. This is a sort of stamp of His being the Eternally-Besought-of-All. Through the tongue of life, every living being recites: *Say: "He is God, the One. God, the Eternally-Besought-of-All"* (112: 1-2).

There are other significant windows or open-ings. I will discuss them briefly. Seeing that each atom opens up three windows and two openings on the Necessarily Existent One's Unity and that life opens two doors, understand how the levels of all beings radiate the light for knowing the All-Majestic One. From this you can understand the degrees of progress in knowledge of God and the degrees of peace attained through it.

FIFTH GLEAM: One pen is enough to write a book by hand. To print it, however, hundreds of metal "pens" must be arranged for each page. Further, if most of the book is to be inscribed in an extremely fine script within certain letters, as *Sura Ya Sin* can (and has been) written within the initial two letters of *Ya* and *Sin*, smaller "pens" are necessary. In the same way, if you accept that this Book of the Universe belongs to the One Who has written it with His Power's Pen, you follow a way so easy as to be necessary and inevitable. But if you attribute it to causality or nature, you follow a way so hard as to be impossible, and so riddled with superstition that even a most fanciful mind could not accept it.

Claiming that nature is self-created means that each soil atom, water drop, and air molecule contains millions of printing machines and innumerable "immaterial factories" [to substitute for Destiny in determining the lives of all things in nature], so that nature could originate all flowering and fruit-bearing plants [and govern their lives]. Or else there should be an all-encompassing knowledge and a power able to do everything in each air, water, and soil atom so that nature really could create itself.

Most plants can grow in any soil if there is enough water and air. But their formation and structure is so systematic, balanced and well-ordered, and their forms are so unique, that a specific factory or "printing machine" would be necessary for each one. To create itself, therefore, nature would need a specific "machine" to create each item. It is very hard to find people who accept such a superstition.

In short, every letter of a book points to itself only to the extent of being a letter and to only one aspect of its existence and meaning. However, it describes its writer and shows him in many ways— for example: "The one who wrote me has fine penmanship. His pen is red." In the same way, each letter of this vast Book of the Universe points to itself to the extent of its size and form, but describes the Eternal Designer's Names as elaborately as an ode, testifies to Him, and points to His Names with its "index fingers" (its qualities). Thus nobody, not even foolish Sophists who deny themselves and the universe, can deny the All-Majestic Maker.

SIXTH GLEAM: Just as the All-Majestic Creator has placed the stamp of His Unity on His creatures' foreheads, He has placed in a most visible fashion many stamps of His Unity on all species, numerous seals of His Unity on all kingdoms of beings, and various signatures of His Oneness on the whole world. Out of these let's look at one placed on Earth's face in spring. This stamp of Divine Unity is as evident and brilliant as spring, during which the Eternal Designer resurrects countless plant and animal species with complete differentiation and specification, and perfect orderliness and separation amid infinite intermingling and confusion.

Is it so hard to perceive that raising dead soil to life in spring, showing with perfect order countless samples of resurrection, and writing on Earth's page the individual members of countless species without fault or forgetting, mistake or deficiency, and in a most well-balanced and well-proportioned, well-ordered and perfect fashion, is a seal unique to One of Majesty, an All-Powerful One of Perfection, an All-Wise One of Grace and Beauty, One Who has infinite Power, all-encompassing Knowledge, and a Will able to govern the universe?

Look upon the signs and imprints of God's Mercy,
how He revives Earth after its death. He will revive
the dead [in the same way]. He is powerful over
all things. (30:50)

Resurrecting the dead is such a simple matter for the Creative Power that, within a few days, gives countless examples of this by quickening Earth. For example, is it proper to ask a miracle-working one who, at a sign, raises up Mount Ararat if he can remove a huge rock blocking your way? In the same way, is it proper to say (in a manner implying doubt) to an All-Wise and Powerful One, an All-Munificent and Compassionate One, Who created the firmaments, Earth and the mountains in "6 days" and continuously fills and empties them: "Can you remove this layer of soil over us that is blocking our way to Your banquet prepared and laid out in eternity? Can you level it and let us pass across it?"

Surely you have seen a stamp of Divine Unity on Earth's face during summer. A seal of Divine Oneness is clearly seen in the most wise, insightful, and mighty Divine operations on Earth's face during spring. This activity is absolutely extensive, speedy, liberal or generous, and done in absolute orderliness. A most perfect beauty of art, it is done in a most perfect form of creation. Thus only One with infinite knowledge and boundless power could own such a seal. That seal belongs to One Who, although nowhere, is all-present and all-seeing. Nothing is hidden from or difficult for Him. With respect to His Power, particles and stars are equal.

Once in a garden of the All-Compassionate One of Grace's munificence, I counted bunches (of grapes) hanging from a grapevine that was two-fingers thick. I saw it to be like one little pip among the "bunches" of His miracles. There were 155 bunches, and one bunch contained about 120 grapes. I thought: If this grape vine were a tap from which honeyed water flowed ceaselessly, only then would the water be enough, in this heat, for the bunches on which hang those hundreds of little "pumps" of mercy's sherbet. But this grapevine manages with only a little moisture, which it occasionally obtains. Therefore the One Who does this must be powerful over all things. Glory be to Him at whose work minds are bewildered.

SEVENTH GLEAM: With a little care and effort, you can see the Eternally-Besought-of-All's seals on Earth's "page." When you raise your head to look at the great Book of the Universe, you will see on it a seal of Divine Unity as big and clear as itself. Like a factory's components or a palace's building blocks, all creatures support, aid, and work together—in perfect orderliness—to meet each other's needs. Joining efforts, they serve living beings. Cooperating, they obey an All-Wise Administrator toward one goal. Obeying the rule of mutual assistance, which is in force throughout the universe, they demonstrate to thoughtful people that they act through the power of a single, Most Munificent Upbringer and at the command of a single, Most Wise Administrator.

Such mutual support and assistance, answering of each other's needs, close cooperation, obedience, submission, and order testify that all creatures are administered through a single Administrator's organization and directed by a single Upbringer. Also, the universal providence and favor included in the universal wisdom, which is clearly apparent in the purposeful creation of things, as well as the comprehensive mercy evident from the providence and the universal sustenance required by that mercy to feed all living beings, form a seal of Divine Unity so brilliant that anyone with sight and thought will see and understand it.

A fabric of wisdom showing intention, consciousness, and will covers the universe; a fine net curtain of providence and favor showing grace, adornment, embellishment, and kindness is placed above it; over that is spread a robe of mercy radiating the will of being known and loved, of favoring with bounties and gifts enveloping the universe; and over that is laid a table of provision for maintaining all creatures, which shows Lordship's kindness, bestowal, benevolence, perfect caring, proper nurturing, grace, and favoring. All of this clearly shows an All-Gracious One Who is All-Wise, All-Generous, All-Compassionate, and All-Providing.

Is everything in need of sustenance? Yes, indeed. Like an individual being needing food to live, all beings, especially living beings, whether universal or particular or wholes or parts, have many material and immaterial demands and needs that must be met if they are to continue living. Although they cannot obtain even the smallest need, we see that all their needs are met, in an unexpected way and from an unexpected source, with perfect order, at the appropriate time, in a suitable fashion, and with perfect wisdom. Does this not clearly show an All-Wise Nurturer of Majesty, an All-Compassionate Provider of Grace?

EIGHTH GLEAM: Seeds sown in a field show that the field and the seeds belong to the one who owns both. Likewise, life's fundamental elements (e.g., air, water, and soil) are universal and omnipresent despite their simplicity and sameness. Plants and animals, which are fruits of Mercy, miracles of Power, and words of Wisdom, also are found everywhere despite their essentially similar nature vis-à-vis life's diverse conditions. This shows that they belong to a single miracle-displaying Maker and that every flower, fruit, and animal is a stamp, a seal, and a signature of that Maker.

Regardless of location, each one proclaims in the tongue of its being: "The One Whose stamp I bear also made this location. The One Whose seal I carry also created this place as a missive. The One Whose signature I indicate also wove this land." Only the One Who holds all elements in His Power's grasp can own and sustain the least of creatures. Those who are not blind can see that only One Who exercises Lordship over all plants and animals can own, sustain, and govern the simplest one of them.

In the tongue of similarity to other individuals, each individual being says: "Only the one who owns my species can own me." In the tongue of spreading over Earth's face with other species, each species says: "Only the one who owns Earth's face can be our owner." In the tongue of being bound to the sun, with other planets, and of its mutual relations with the heavens, Earth says: "Only the one who owns all these can be my owner."

Suppose apples were conscious and that someone said to one of them: "You are my work of art." The apple would exclaim: "Be quiet! If you can form all apples on Earth; rather, if you have power over all fruit-bearing trees on Earth and over all the gifts of the All-Merciful One proceeding from the treasury of Mercy, only then can you claim Lordship over me!"

NINTH GLEAM: After pointing out some of the seals, stamps, and signatures on particulars and parts, universals and wholes, as well as on the world, life, living beings, and on the giving of life, I will indicate one of the countless stamps on species.

Since a tree's countless fruits depend on one law of growth from one center, they are as easy and cheap to raise as a single fruit. In other words, multiple centers would require for a single fruit as much hardship, expenditure, and equipment as for a whole tree, and manufacturing the needed military equipment for one soldier would require all factories for a whole army. The first case explains the extraordinary ease of creating all species from a center of unity; the second case shows the impossible and countless difficulties that arise if creation were dependent upon multiple centers.

In short, therefore, the correspondence and similarity in basic members between a species' members and a genus' divisions proves that they are works of a single Maker, as they are "inscribed" with the same Pen and bear the same seal. The absolute ease of their creation, which makes them necessary and inevitable, requires that they be the work of One Maker. Otherwise, the ensuing difficulties would doom that genus and that species to non-existence.

Given this, attributing everything to Almighty God makes all things are as easy as one thing; when attributed to causes, one thing is impossibly difficult. Thus the extraordinary economy and ease seen in the universe, as well as the endless abundance, clearly show the stamp of Unity. If these abundant and cheap fruits did not belong to the One of Unity, we could not buy a pomegranate even if we gave the world in exchange. How could we pay for the purposeful and conscious cooperation of the various universal elements (e.g., soil, air, water, sunlight, heat) and the seed, all of which are unconscious and obey a Single Maker, Who is Almighty God? The cost of a pomegranate or any other fruit is the whole universe.

TENTH GLEAM: Just as life, which manifests Divine Grace, is an argument and proof for Divine Unity, even a sort of manifestation of Divine Unity, death, which manifests Divine Majesty, is an argument and proof for Divine Oneness.[37]

---

[37] Oneness (Ahadiya) and Unity (Wahidiya) differ. Oneness means the concurrent manifestations of all or most of the Divine Names on one thing. For example, life is the result of the manifestations of many Names, such as the Creator, Fashioner, All-Favoring, All-Merciful, and All-Providing. Unity means the manifestation of a Divine Name on all things, as death is common to all living beings and results from the manifestation of the Divine Name the One-Who-Causes-To-Die. (Tr.)

Consider this: Bubbles on a mighty river reflect the sun's image and light, as do transparent objects glistening on Earth's face. Both testify to the sun's existence. Although the bubbles sometimes disappear (such as by passing under a bridge), successive troops of bubbles continue to show the sun's reflection and display its light. This proves that the little images of the sun, which appear, disappear, and then re-appear, point to an enduring, perpetual, single sun that continues to manifest itself from on high. Thus, those sparkling bubbles demonstrate the sun's existence and display its continuation and unity through their disappearance and extinction.

In the same way, the existence and life of these beings in continuous flux testify to the Necessarily Existent Being's necessary Existence and Oneness, as well as to His Unity, eternity, and permanence, via their decay and death. The beautiful, delicate creatures that are renewed and recruited along, with the alternation of day and night, summer and winter, and the passage of centuries and ages, show the Existence, Unity, and permanence of an elevated, everlasting One with a continuous display of beauty.

In the same way, their decay and death, together with the apparent causes for their lives, show that (material or natural) causes are only veils. This proves that these arts, inscriptions, and manifestations are the constantly renewed arts, changing inscriptions, and moving mirrors of an All-Beautiful One of Majesty, all of Whose Names are sacred and beautiful. Also, they are His stamps that follow one after the other, and His seals that are charged with wisdom.

This Book of the Universe instructs us in the signs of Divine Existence and Unity seen in the universe's creation and operation, and bears witness to all the All-Majestic One's Attributes of Perfection, Beauty, Grace, and Majesty. These signs also prove the essential Perfection of Divine Being, without fault and defect, for a work's perfection points to the perfection of the act lying in that work's origin. The act's perfection points to the name's perfection, which points to the attribute's perfection, which points to the essential capacity's perfection, which necessarily, intuitively, and evidently points to the perfection of the one with that essential capacity.

For example, a perfect palace's perfect design and adornments show the perfection of a master-builder's acts. The acts' perfection show the perfection of the eminent builder's titles, which specify his rank. The titles' perfection show the perfection of the builder's attributes, which are the origin of the art. The perfection of the art and attributes show the perfection of the master's abilities and essential capacity. The perfection of those essential abilities and capacity show the perfection of the master's essential nature.

In the same way, the faultless works seen in the universe, about which the Qur'an asks: *Do you see any flaw?* (67:3), the art in the universe's well-ordered beings, point to an Effective, Powerful Agent's perfect acts. The acts' perfection point to the perfection of that Majestic Agent's Names. The Names' perfection points and testifies to the perfection of the Attributes of the Majestic One known with the Names. The Attributes' perfection points and testifies to the perfection of the essential capacity and qualities of the Perfect One qualified by those attributes. The perfection of the essential capacity and qualities point to the perfection of the One having such capacity and qualities with such certainty that all types of perfections observed throughout the universe are but signs of His Perfection, hints of His Majesty, and allusions to His Beauty in the forms of pale, weak shadows when compared to His Perfect Reality.

ELEVENTH GLEAM AS RADIANT AS THE SUN: As shown in The Nineteenth Word, our master Muhammad the Trustworthy is the supreme "verse" of the great Book of the Universe, the "Greatest Name" of God manifested in that "Qur'an" of the cosmos, the seed and most illustrious fruit of the Tree of Creation, the sun of the palace of the world, the luminous full moon of the world of Islam, and the herald of Divine Lordship's sovereignty. He is the wise discoverer of creation's secret, the one who flies through the levels of truth on the wings of Messengership, which embraces all previous Prophets, and of Islam, which takes under its protection the world of Islam. With the support of all Prophets and Messengers, saints and truthful, truth-seeking scholars and purified ones, he attested to Divine Unity with all his strength and opened the way to the Divine Throne. What fancy or doubt can divert belief in God, which he demonstrated, and close this way to Divine Unity, which he proved?

Since I described, to some extent, that clear proof and miracle-working being through 14 droplets from the water of life of his knowledge in The Nineteenth Word, and through 19 signs in The Nineteenth Letter (on his miracles), I conclude with calling God's blessing on him as testimony to his truthfulness.

> O God, bestow blessings on the one who leads to the necessity of Your Existence and Your Unity, and testifies to Your Majesty and Grace and Perfection; the truthful and confirmed witness, and the verified, articulate proof; the lord of Prophets and Messengers, the bearer of the meaning of their consensus, affirmation, and miracles; the leader of saints and fruitful ones, who has the meaning of their agreement, verifications, and wonder-working; and the one with evident miracles, clear wonders, and decisive proofs that corroborate and affirm him.

> [O God, bestow blessings on] the one with exalted virtues in his person, elevated morals in his duty, and lofty qualities in his Shari'a, perfect and free of all contradiction; the center where Divine Revelation descended, as agreed upon by the One Who revealed, what was revealed, and the one who brought the Revelation to him; the traveler

through the worlds of the Unseen and the inner dimensions of things; the observer of spirits, who conversed with angels; and the sample of all the perfections in creation, in regard to individuals, species, and genera (the Tree of Creation's most illustrious fruit).

[O God, bestow blessings on] the lamp of truth, the proof of reality, the embodiment of mercy, the model of love, the discoverer of the secret of creation, the herald of the sovereignty of Divine Lordship, the one who demonstrated through the sublimity of his spiritual personality that he was before the "eyes" of the Author of the World at the creation of the universe, and the one who brought a Shari'a that shows through the comprehensiveness and soundness of its principles that it is the order of the Composer of the world and established by the Creator of the universe.

The One Who composed the universe with this perfect order composed this religion [Islam] with its finest and most beautiful order. He is our master, master of the communities of the children of Adam; our guide to belief, the communities of believers, Muhammad ibn 'Abd Allah ibn 'Abd al-Muttalib, upon him be the best of blessings and the most perfect peace as long as Earth and the heavens subsist. As the leader of all other witnesses and instructor of all human generations, this truthful and confirmed witness witnessed and announced with all his strength, utmost solemnity, utter steadfastness, strength of certainty, and perfection of belief: "I bear witness that there is no god but God, the One. He has no partner."

TWELFTH GLEAM AS RADIANT AS THE SUN: This twelfth gleam is such an ocean of truths that all 22 Words are only 22 drops in it. It is such a source of light that they are only 22 rays in it. Each Word is only a ray from one of the stars of the verses shining in the heavens of the Qur'an. Each is a drop from the river of a verse flowing from that Ocean of the Distinguisher between Truth and Falsehood, a pearl from a verse, each of which is a chest of jewels in the greatest of treasuries: God's Book.

This word of God is defined a little in the 14 droplet of The Nineteenth Word. Originating in the Greatest Name of God, it descended from the Supreme Divine Throne as the greatest manifestation of Divine Lordship. So elevated and comprehensive as to encompass and then even transcend time and bind the ground to the Supreme Divine Throne, it repeatedly declares with all its strength and its verses' absolute certainty: "There is no god but God." Making the universe testify to this, all of its contents sing in unison: "There is no god but God."

If you look at the Qur'an with the eyes of a sound heart, you will see that its six sides are so brilliant and transparent that no darkness and misguidance, doubt and suspicion, or deception can penetrate it. Nor is there a fissure through which such things could infiltrate into the sphere of its purity. Above it is the stamp of miraculousness, beneath it proof and evidence, behind it its point of support—pure Divine Revelation, before it happiness in this world and the next, on its right questioning human reason about its truth and ensuring its confirmation, and on its left calling the human conscience to testify to its truth and securing its submission. In its inside is the pure guidance of the All-Merciful One, and on its outside is the light of belief.

Its fruits, with the certainty depending on observation, are the purified and truth-loving scholars and saints, adorned with all human perfections and attainments. If you listen to that Tongue of the Unseen—the Qur'an—you will hear from its depths a most familiar and convincing, an infinitely solemn and elevated, heavenly voice furnished with proofs that declares repeatedly: "There is no god but He." It states this with such absolute certainty depending on actual experience and complete conviction, that, concerning its truth, it gives you certainty of knowledge to the degree of the certainty coming from direct witnessing and observation.

In short, the Messenger and the Most Firm Criterion to distinguish between truth and falsehood (the Qur'an) are each a "sun." The former, the tongue of the visible, material world, along with the support of 1,000 miracles and confirmation of all Prophets and purified scholars, points with the fingers of Islam and Messengership to the truth of "There is no god but God" and shows it with all his strength. The latter, the tongue of the Unseen world, having 40 aspects of miraculousness and confirmed by creation's Divine signs and the universe's operation, points to the same truth with the fingers of right and guidance, and shows it in a most solemn manner. Thus that truth is clearer than the sun and more manifest than daylight.

O obstinate one immersed in misguidance, who attempts to deny and annul the Qur'an! How can you oppose these suns with your mind's dim lamp?

How can you remain indifferent? Are you trying to extinguish them by blowing? Enough of your denying mind! How can you deny the words and claims spoken by the Qur'an and the Prophet in the Name of the Lord of all the worlds and Owner of the universe? Who are you that you attempt to deny the Majestic Owner of the universe?

Conclusion

O friend with an alert mind and an attentive heart. If you have understood this Word, take these 12 gleams in your hand so that you might obtain a lamp of truth as light-giving as thousands of electric lights. Hold fast to the Qur'anic verses descending from God's Supreme Throne. Climbing on the "mount" of Divine assistance, ascend to the heavens of truth. Rise to the "throne of Divine knowledge" and declare: "I bear witness that there is no god but You. You are One, without partner."

Also declare:

> There is no god but God, One, having no partner; His is the dominion of all existence, and to Him belongs all praise; He alone gives life and causes to die; He is living and dies not; in His hand is all good; and He is powerful over everything. Glory be to You. We have no knowledge save what You have

taught us. Truly, you are the All-Knowing, the All-Wise.

Our Lord, do not call us to account if we forget or fall into error. Our Lord, do not lay on us a burden like that which You laid on those before us. Our Lord, do not impose on us that which we cannot bear. Pardon us, forgive us, and have mercy on us. You are our Protector. Give us victory over the people of disbelief. Our Lord, do not cause our hearts to swerve after You have guided us. Bestow upon us mercy from Your Presence, for You are the Bestower. Our Lord, You are He who will gather humanity together on a Day of which there is no doubt. God never fails in His promise.

O God, bestow blessings and peace on the one whom You sent as a mercy for all the worlds, and on his Family and Companions. Have mercy on us and his community, for the sake of Your Mercy, O most Merciful of the Merciful. Amen.

The conclusion of their call will be: "All praise be to God, the Lord of the Worlds."

Index

A

Abraham (Prophet), 38, 65
Adam (Prophet), 12, 128

B

Beauty (Divine), 9, 10, 13, 48, 100, 114, 116, 123, 124, 126
belief, 2, 11, 12, 67, 70, 95, 96, 126, 128, 129, 130

C

cause and effect, 32, 46, 59, 98, 99
companions, 39, 61, 62, 69, 133
compassion, 6, 8, 61, 82

D

death, 8, 9, 35, 36, 37, 38, 39, 43, 65, 74, 75, 76, 78, 79, 81, 85, 87, 88, 89, 90, 91, 93, 100, 101, 102, 109, 115, 122, 123, 124
desire, 28, 41, 45
Destiny, 15, 20, 21, 46, 57, 74, 75, 76, 78, 108, 112

E

enlightenment, 2, 95
eternal life, 9, 35, 37

eternity, 8, 19, 20, 22, 33, 38, 115, 123
evil, 3

F

falsehood, 12, 129, 131
forgiveness, 62
freedom, 46

G

generosity, 8, 26, 50
goodness, 9
gratitude, 33
grave, 10, 14, 66
guidance, 58, 95, 130, 131

H

heart, 2, 3, 62, 102, 103, 130, 132
Hell, 56, 65
Hereafter, 3, 19, 31, 61

I

Ibn al-'Arabi, 54
illusion, 54
immortal, 8
impotence, 11, 32, 39, 60, 110
intention, 45, 118

J

jinn, 2, 9, 10, 60

justice, 17, 61

L

love, 2, 6, 9, 13, 32, 33, 74, 75, 76, 78, 79, 81, 85, 87, 88, 89, 90, 91, 93, 95, 128

M

miracle, 30, 44, 74, 77, 78, 84, 86, 91, 92, 93, 115, 119, 127

N

non-existence, 8, 14, 37, 54, 59, 121

P

Paradise, 11, 12, 13, 14, 47, 52, 56, 59, 60, 62
philosophy, 15, 16
Plato, 15, 16
poverty, 15, 39, 40
prayer, 74, 75, 76, 78, 79, 81, 85, 87, 88, 89, 90, 91, 93
Prophets, 60, 126, 127, 131
punishment, 88
purpose, 6, 17, 32, 36, 42, 45

R

reason, 5, 52, 89, 99, 102, 130
reflection, 10, 27, 53, 54, 104, 105, 123
repentance, 62

Resurrection, 34, 47, 56, 60, 114
Revelation, 61, 127, 130
reward, 10, 11

S

saints, 60, 126, 127, 130
science, 108
Scriptures, 60
self, 8, 33, 34, 35, 59, 64, 103, 110, 112
selfhood, 82
sin, 112
soul, 23, 58, 63
spirit, 2, 3, 4, 5, 33

U

unbelief, 74, 75, 76, 78, 79, 81, 85, 87, 88, 89, 90
Unity (Divine), 1, 3, 5, 7, 9, 11, 13, 14, 15, 17, 19, 20, 21, 23, 25, 27, 28, 29, 31, 33, 35, 37, 39, 41, 43, 45, 47, 48, 49, 51, 52, 53, 55, 57, 59, 61, 63, 65, 67, 69, 71, 74, 75, 76, 78, 79, 81, 85, 87, 88, 89, 90, 95, 96, 97, 98, 100, 108, 110, 114, 115, 117, 118, 122, 126, 127

W

worship, 3, 9, 11, 14, 20, 22, 29, 31, 32, 33